Super Massage

SIMPLE TECHNIQUES FOR INSTANT RELAXATION

GORDON INKELES

PIATKUS

This edition first published in Great Britain in 1989 by Judy Piatkus (Publishers) Ltd of 5 Windmill Street, London W1

Reprinted 1989
Reprinted 1990

Printed and bound in Great Britain by Butler & Tanner Ltd, Frome and London

British Library Cataloguing-in-Publication Data

Inkeles, Gordon
    Super Massage.
    1. Physical fitness. Relaxation.
      Massage
    I. Title
    613.7′9

ISBN 0-86188-827-8
ISBN 0-86188-832-4 pbk

Designed and produced by Jon Goodchild/Triad.
Photographed by Gordon Inkeles
Illustrations by Sigga Bjornsson

Acknowledgments

I am grateful to Lee Wakefield, who said "everyone you meet is looking for a way to *unwind*," and to Iris Schencke, who simply said "yes."

I particularly want to acknowledge the following models in these pages: Ringit Gurlich, Chris Tesser, Yvonne Armstrong, Lars Tragardh, Laura McCauley, Alex Bratenahl, Joseph James, Claire Iris, David Mohrmann . . . and Little. And special thanks to Margaret Brown, to the Bourassa and Knapp families, who offered their homes for photography, to my editor, Susan Victor, to designer Tarané Saylor, and to my grip, Scott Harrison, who did all the photo processing.

This book was photographed with a motorized Nikon F-3 using focal lengths of 35 to 180 mm. With the exception of the Insomnia chapter, which was shot in San Francisco, all of the pictures were taken in the natural winter light of Humboldt County, California.

Always consult a doctor if yo are in doubt about a medical condition, and observe the cautions given in the book.

To my mother,
Alice Taft Inkeles

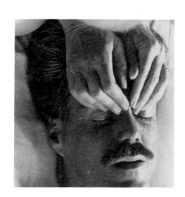 

Other books by Gordon Inkeles

The Art of Sensual Massage

The New Massage

Massage and Peaceful Pregnancy

Contents

Preface

This is a book for hardworking people who want to remain relaxed and healthy. What follows is not a complete health plan but it is, perhaps, the missing element in the plan you've been practicing. Have you tried exercising, diets, and self-improvement programs only to find that stress remains a major problem in your life? The smug Puritan may insist, "There's no gain without pain," but in massage we have another idea: you should be able to be busy and productive without suffering from constant stress. And without hurting.

This is not a self-help program. When dealing with stress, almost any kind of self-help is futile because *most seriously stressed individuals cannot help themselves relax.* Exercise, meditation, and hobbies too often become obsessive and competitive, transforming what should have been a relaxing experience into a stressful ordeal. Thinking rationally about stress (or trying hard not to think about it) just makes it worse. Help has to come from outside, from other people.

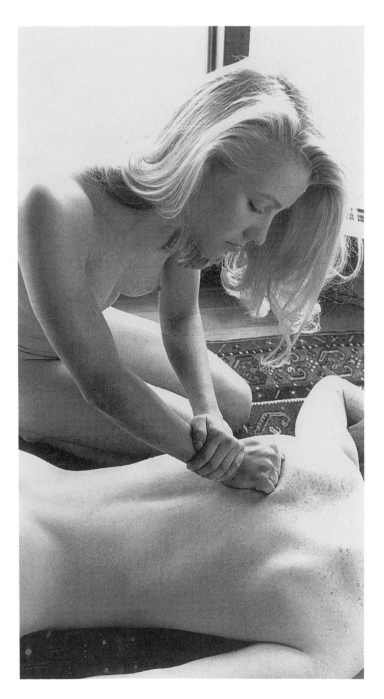

Massage is drugless stress control. To the executive it means quick energy boosts and a way to cut through fatigue, to the athlete it offers sensational muscle recovery rates after exercise, to the insomniac it brings peace, and to the lover, a new way of touching. It can also provide a simple but amazingly effective facial. Taken regularly, massage can change one's life.

All of the techniques in this book are easy to learn and they all work in minutes. My hope is that you will now open the book to any page and try massage on a willing partner. The results? In minutes you will see stress-induced pain vanish as pure pleasure takes its place. That's one of the things human hands can do; ease pain. But that's only the beginning.

January 1988
Miranda, California

Introduction

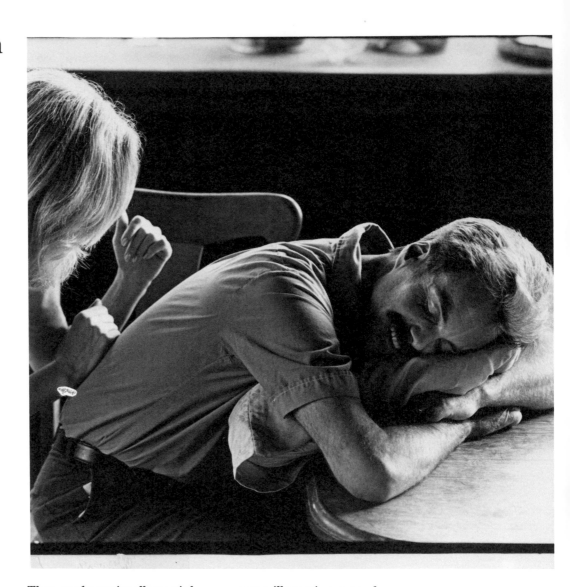

There are the continually wearied, wakeful, and nervous business or professional men with numerous and varying ailments, who have learned by experience that "the labor they delight in physics pain," and who find more relief in work than in rest. Mas-sage will sometimes put such on a higher plane of existence and give them a zest for work which they have not derived from any other source.
— Douglas Graham, M.D.,
A Treatise on Massage

The Seduction of Stress

Have you resigned yourself to living with stress? Do you experience daily soreness around the neck and shoulders, aching feet, headaches, lower back problems? Do you have trouble falling asleep? Does exercise leave your body aching for hours? You're not alone. Nonspecific aches and pains are now one of the main complaints in hospital emergency rooms all over the country. Perhaps you've checked with a doctor and discovered that nothing's seriously wrong with you — you're just under a lot of pressure. But isn't every successful individual under a lot of pressure and in a hurry? Must one, then, simply find a way to live with nonspecific pain?

If you accept high stress levels as inevitable, you adjust to various stresses rather than avoiding them; you take pride in the ability to squeeze that extra ounce of effort out, no matter what the cost to the nervous system. And if stress is inevitable, so is pain.

Of course, days with no stress whatsoever would be relentlessly dull — a stimulating life should help you stay healthy into your seventies and eighties. But to remain productive, happy and relaxed in the modern world you need an effective way of controlling stress; you need to find a way to unwind. You can't afford to fool around with drugs; the side effects are too costly. You've had it with toothless self-help programs; you want to feel better right now, not three months from now. You're committed to your career — imagine how much you could accomplish if you were able to work hard without hurting.

Unwinding with Super Massage

Forget the thirty-day program or the regimen of costly therapy—overstressed people deserve a much quicker solution. The techniques in this book work in *minutes*, not days, weeks, or months.

Practiced everywhere on earth since Biblical times, massage is the most ancient form of stress control; it is the original medical tool. The Super Massage program is designed to cut through stress and bring relaxation fast. As you begin to use it, you will learn to recognize the warning signs of excessive stress and take action. On every part of the body you can do things with massage that your partner simply cannot do for himself. High stress levels are accompanied by ominous chemical changes inside the body. These too are reversible with Super Massage. Many of the techniques described in this book are designed to penetrate deep within the body and reach hidden sources of stress. You'll also learn to analyze the chemistry of fatigue and purge the body of acidic irritants that keep the muscles perpetually tensed.

At the heart of the Super Massage program is the amazing fluid release effect, a massage technique that alters, in minutes, the chemistry of

fatigue and stress. The fluid release effect adapts a technique that is employed by Olympic trainers, allowing stressed parts of the body to be super oxygenated while irritating acidic wastes are pressed out of the tissues.

The results simply have to be experienced to be believed: nagging aches and pains disappear, fatigue vanishes, and a sense of well-being takes its place. After fifteen minutes of fluid release massage, muscle recovery rates double and work output increases by more than 100 percent.[*] Massive increases in red and white blood cells are noted in the massaged areas, and oxygen levels also jump. Perhaps most significantly, irritating acidic wastes that would normally linger in the tissues for days, even weeks, are dispersed in minutes.[†] There is, simply, no way outside of massage to duplicate these astonishing effects.

Massage allows people to feel instead of think. It immediately brings relaxation to tensed muscles, reversing the

[*]Douglas Graham, M.D., *Massage: Manual Treatment, Remedial Movements* (Philadelphia: Lippincott, 1913), p.83.

[†]Hermann Bucholtz, *Therapeutic Exercise and Massage* (Philadelphia and New York: Lea & Febiger, 1920), p. 122.

tendency of stress to create more stress. It eases pain without resorting to drugs. It calms the nerves and stimulates circulation. And it works every time.

Super Massage techniques feel very good and that, too, is part of the program. In

massage, pleasure itself is therapeutic. The astonishing changes that occur during Super Massage—spectacular muscle recovery rates and extended endurance—have been documented by scientists only recently but the techniques have been tested for thousands of years.

Modern scientists have provided the evidence that the ancients took for granted. A hundred years ago massage enjoyed a renaissance as an accepted medical treatment for rheumatism, gout, sprains, nervous tension, fatigue, and a number of other afflictions. At the turn of the century the medical community looked on with great interest when a Dutch physician named Metzger chose to massage the chronically aching joints of Denmark's sickly prince. His highness's renewed interest in skiing, just one week after the massage began, brought eager students to Amsterdam from all over Europe (among them, the prince's personal physician) to study Metzger's methods. At the same time, scientists became intensely interested in the remarkable powers of massage. Embraced by healers for centuries, the practice would finally be tested in the laboratory.

First, the experimenters tried to find out what actually happened inside the body during massage. In Philadelphia, Dr. Weir-Mitchell injected the thigh muscles of two rabbits with India ink, then let them run around as usual. One rabbit was massaged regularly, the other not at all. After two weeks the India ink in the rabbit that was not massaged had spread to surrounding tissues, staining them a deep black. But in the rabbit that was massaged there was no trace of India ink anywhere in the body! Urinalysis of human subjects confirmed the findings: a higher concentration of toxins was expelled from the body up to one full week after a single massage.*

But there were even more dramatic changes ahead. Dr. Weir-Mitchell had written a book called *Fat and Blood* in which he examined the chemistry of fatigue and speculated on its causes. Portions of the body, he said, become stagnant either through disuse or constant tension, then diseased. Stagnant tissues, packed with irritating wastes, became tense and tended to remain that way, resisting the effects of exercise and various drugs.

*Dr. Emil A.G. Kleen, *Massage and Medical Gymnastics* (London: J.A. Churchill, 1918), p. 69.

Unwinding with Super Massage (cont'd)

Would massage help? The experimenters noted an elevated red and white corpuscle count immediately after massage, which meant that fresh oxygen was being pumped into the tissues. In oxygenated parts of the body, trapped gasses, acids, and toxins that kept muscles tense began to burn off, leaving stagnant tissues refreshed after a single massage. During the stroking, wastes that didn't combust were squeezed out of the muscles and finally eliminated from the body as surely as the India ink in the massaged rabbit's thigh. Acidic irritants and toxins that usually lingered for days actually vanished in minutes.

But the most amazing data of all emerged from studies of fatigued muscles, which were conducted almost simultaneously in Italy, Germany, and the United States. Normally, muscle recovery rates five minutes after exercise are about 20 percent. But when five minutes of massage was substituted for the five minutes of rest, muscle recovery rates greater than 100 percent were recorded.*

Douglas Graham, the great American physician who devoted his life to massage, immediately began testing the new findings on his patients. He found that just five minutes of massage would restore a specific muscle group as well as two hours of sleep; ten minutes of massage had the same effect as a whole night's rest!† One didn't have to endure fatigue all day long; there was an alternative.

With the discovery of antibiotics and modern painkillers, however, massage abruptly lost favor in medical circles. The evidence was in: massage could alter the chemistry of fatigue; it could relieve pain and relax tensed muscles in minutes. But now there were pills that seemed to do the same thing even faster. Overworked doctors welcomed a deluge of "mira-

cle drugs," overlooking, for the time being, their ominous side effects. It became more cost effective to knock out the whole central nervous system to cure a headache than to massage a patient for five minutes. A few Olympic-class athletes continued to use massage as a kind of secret weapon (most notably, runners Waldemar Cierpinski and Alberto Salazar, world record holder in the marathon from 1969 to 1982). But for most people massage became a rare luxury to be sampled only by the rich and powerful.

In fact, some of the most pressured characters in history — Julius Caesar, Cleopatra, Louis XV, Ulysses S. Grant, Ivan the Terrible, Indira Gandhi, Bob Hope, Marlene Dietrich, and Henry Kissinger, to name just a few — seldom left home without a masseur. They understood that massage can make the extraordinary physical and emotional strains of leadership bearable. A good masseur can relax almost anyone. Now you can, too.

*Professor J.B. Zabludowski, "Über die physiologische Bedeutung der Massage," *Centralblatt für die Med. Wissenschaften*, April 7, 1883 (in Graham, *Massage: Manual Treatment, Remedial Movements*, p.82). Professor Maggioria, *Archives Italiene de Biologie* (University of Turin), Tome XVL, fasc. ii-iii (in Graham, *Massage: Manual Treatment, Remedial Movements*, p.85). *American Journal of the Sciences*, May 1894 (in Graham, *Massage: Manual Treatment, Remedial Movements*, p.93). W.S. Playfair, M.D., *Nerve Prostration and Hysteria* (London: King's College), p.85 (in Graham, *Massage: Manual Treatment, Remedial Movements*, p. 118).

†Harvey Kellogg, M.D., *A Practical Manual for the Nurse, the Student, and the Practitioner* (Battle Creek, Michigan: Modern Medicine Publishing Co., 1929), p. 273.

1.
Inside the Body: The Power of Super Massage

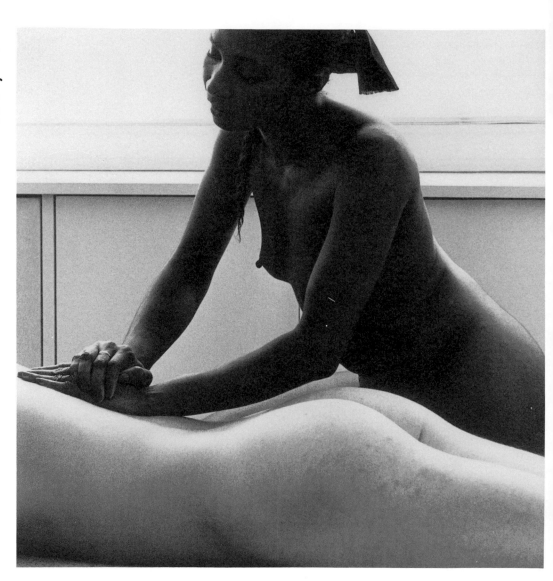

The ideal stress-control technique would:

☛ Remove acidic irritants from the tissues.

☛ Oxygenate the whole area.

☛ Not speed up the heart

☛ Not depend on a drug.

☛ Work in less than five minutes.

The Amazing Fluid Release Effect:
How You Can Use It to Control Stress

Reach down to man's most atavistic levels, and release the automatic tensions that make him a slave to his own boredom and to the world around him.
—Colin Wilson, *The Mind Parasites*

It's tempting to conclude that stressed people are suffering from purely psychological problems. Can one then explain, rationally, to the stressed individual that constant nervousness, snappish behavior, and trouble concentrating are destructive? Probably not. Medical research has determined that stress is often caused by biological agents deep within the body. That's why you can't control the wild mood swings and mysterious ailments with rational thinking, positive thinking, or any other kind of thinking. You have to go directly to the body.

Where does stress begin? Every muscle, skin, and nerve cell requires a constant supply of oxygen and nutrients in order to function properly. Cells are literally bathed in blood-soluble nutrients every moment of the day and night. Inside the cells these nutrients combine with oxy-

INSTANT BENEFITS:

Circulation

Interior oxygen level boosted
Heart rested
Blood pressure lowered
Vascular and lymphatic toning

Muscles

Muscles recover from fatigue more than 300 percent faster!
Increased endurance

Nerves and brain

Immediate relaxation
Wrinkle and worry lines recede
Relief from cramps
Diminished anxiety and nervous tension

Skin and hair

Removes dead skin
Moisturizes the hair

gen and then combust to produce life-sustaining energy. Stress is created when the exhaust gasses, toxins, and wastes produced by combustion remain within the cell. Deep within the body chemical concentrations that trigger stress must be released from the cells before real relaxation is possible. When stress is viewed as a *chemical* phenomenon rather than a purely mental one, the tremendous potential of fluid release massage becomes clear.

We all agree that stressed people can become terribly irritating; however, their tendency to attack others is mirrored within. The stressed individual is under relentless attack from inside his own body by powerful acids and poisons. Normally, most toxins are expelled from internal tissues via the intricate capillary and lymphatic systems whose vessels are no more than a fraction of a centimeter in diameter. But when the body reacts to a stressful situation, the entire vascular and lymphatic system abruptly contracts. At the same time, the blood supply to interior tissues is sharply reduced. As the oxygen rate declines, nearby muscles tighten, pressing hard against the interior lymph and blood vessels.

Fluid Release Effect (cont'd)

During the massive vaso-constriction that follows, major blood vessels are often visibly contracted. Smaller ones sometimes close down altogether, blocking nearly all waste dispersal from the surrounding tissues. Irritating acidic wastes then begin to accumulate in the tissues, and the classic vicious cycle of stress is complete: the wastes produce tension, the tension produces more vaso-constriction, which in turn causes more acidic wastes to collect in the tissues. Relaxation becomes difficult because the muscles, constantly irritated from within, will not let go. In the end, the stressed individual is poisoned by his own wastes.

Vigorous exercise, the holy grail of the overstressed, can easily make the whole situation worse. Blood circulation is temporarily boosted, only to have large quantities of a new irritating waste, called lactic acid, pumped into the tissues. One must do less to be free of stress, not more.

The amazing massage technique called the fluid release effect, developed and widely tested (most recently on Olympic athletes), actually counters the effects of stress. In fluid release massage we concentrate on opening the intricate capillary and lymphatic systems that wastes

must pass through to get out of the body. Masseurs deal with stress as a physical problem and seek to restore tranquility by creating gentle changes inside the body. During fluid release massage an intense cleansing process begins at the cellular level.

Recently, a team of scientists set out to analyze the effects of various strokes by measuring the precise chemical content of wastes expelled from the body before and after a massage. After dozens of chemicals had been monitored, two dramatic changes in body chemistry, indicating

how extraordinarily powerful massage could be as a stress control agent, emerged. The scientists found that when tensed muscles relaxed their grip on the fragile lymphatic vessels, adrenaline, perhaps the most stressful chemical of all, was suddenly expelled from the body at a rate 50 percent faster than normal. Expulsion of histamine, the nasty stuff that cold and allergy remedies try so hard to vanquish, was accelerated by a phenomenal 129 percent![*] Fluid release massage, it turned out, had a selective tranquilizing effect that no

drug could match; somehow, *just the chemicals that actually cause stress were pressed out of the tissues and expelled from the body.*

As wastes are pressed out of the cells, the capillary and venous systems are opened and, simultaneously, great quantities of oxygen and nutrients are pumped into the tissues. The result? Your partner will rise from the massage feeling refreshed, calm, and curiously energized.

---

[*]W. Kurz and G. Wittlinger, *Angiology* 10 (1978), pp. 764–72.

Benefits to Circulation

After five minutes of Super Massage, the oxygen content of all massaged tissues has increased from 10 to 15 percent. Saturating the tissues with oxygen-rich blood provides a kind of natural analgesic—everything that hurts, hurts less. Inside the body even more dramatic changes are taking place. Massage cannot manufacture blood cells, but it can direct existing quantities to a specific area.

Repeating a simple circulation movement for five minutes boosts the white blood cell count in the massaged area by 85 percent. At the same time it increases local blood flow without straining your partner's heart and circulatory system. In fact, while you massage, your partner's pulse rate will actually decline as the heart pumps more slowly.

When you give a Super Massage, your hands take over some of the work that is usually done by your partner's heart. The vascular system is toned, blood pressure drops, and the heart is rested. Again, these effects cannot be reproduced, all at once, outside of massage.

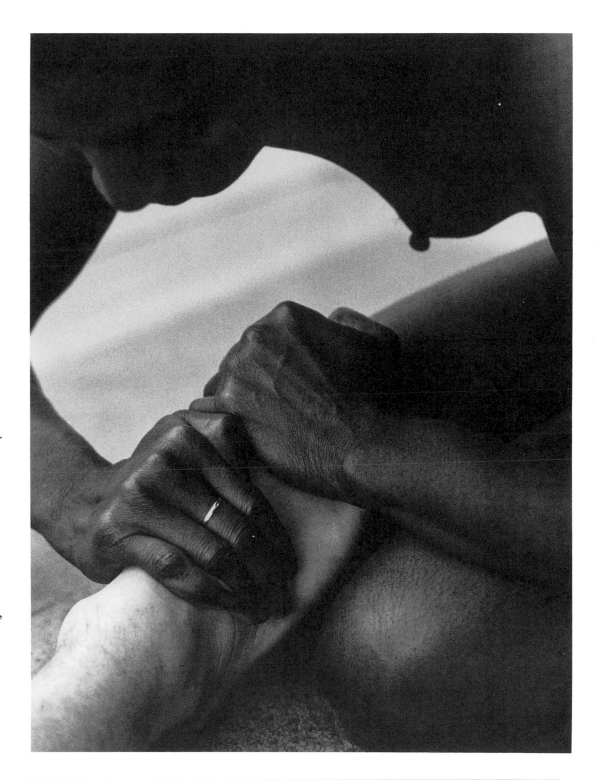

Benefits to Muscles

Recently, professional athletes and trainers have become fascinated with the astonishing muscle recovery rates that have been recorded after just a few minutes of fluid release massage. Although the original experiments were done by medical people at the turn of the century, their results were ignored for decades by an antitactile society.

Athletes became seriously interested in fluid release massage when they realized it offers a way to dramatically reduce muscle fatigue. In sports where extended muscle endurance is required, massage is now considered indispensable. Cyclists competing in endurance races like the Tour de France and the Giro de Italia, which call for sprints of more than one hundred miles a day, simply cannot compete without massage. *Runner's World* author Ray Hosler emphasizes just how crucial massage becomes in cycle marathons where "the legs take incredible punishment and the buildup of lactic acid is inordinate. Were a professional to be without his daily leg massage, he would soon find himself slipping in the standings." Recently, Alberto Salazar

revealed his secret: a twice-weekly massage session which permitted him to commit to a phenomenal seventeen-week training schedule with no breaks! Salazar is convinced that he couldn't have achieved his world records without the massage.*

What, precisely, can fluid release techniques do for fatigued muscles? Normally, the muscle recovery rate after exercise is slightly less than 20 percent. An individual capable of doing a hundred sit-ups has recovered enough

energy, after five minutes of rest, to do no more than twenty additional sit-ups (a 20 percent recovery rate). But if we completely eliminate the rest period and substitute five minutes of fluid release massage, the muscle recovery rates increase to between 75 percent and 125 percent! It was this astonishing performance jump that attracted the interest of U.S. Olympic trainers, who now follow the

example of the East Germans and include massage in almost all sports training. But the full ramifications of the amazing muscle recovery rates after Super Massage extend far beyond athletics. Who can say what any of us would be capable of if we could work three times as hard before getting tired?

*Ray Hosler, *Runner's World Massage Book* (Mountain View, California: Runner's World Books, 1982), p. 186.

Benefits to the Nerves and Brain

The first step in controlling wrinkles is to soothe the nerves that supply the facial muscles. The same acids that clog muscle cells deposit microscopic debris on the nerves.*

Nerve debris interferes with electrical transmission, creating a disturbance that is communicated directly to the muscles. Probably the most mood-sensitive part of the body is the area around the mouth and eyes, where the tiny muscles of expression are shaped. Here, nervous tension simply cannot be hidden; the skin wrinkles visibly with every mood change. Relax the nerves that supply the face and your partner's expression is transformed, sometimes while you're massaging. Suddenly the face appears more natural and composed, as though unnecessary lines have been eliminated. They have. Very often, fully half of the visible wrinkles are nothing more than "tension tracks" that

disappear without a trace after five minutes of Super Massage.

On other parts of the body deeper nerves are more pressure-sensitive. Light to moderate pressures during massage are stimulating; heavy pressures have a sedative effect. A woman's nerves are more sensitive to touch than a man's.

Cramped muscles can sometimes be traced to irritated nerves. Direct pressure, with compression strokes (see p. 50), on the nerves that supply the cramped muscle will sometimes relieve the cramp.

Although the brain itself cannot feel, it can be massaged indirectly via the nerves. Soothe the nerves and your partner's anxieties begin to vanish. Again, in massage we deal with emotional or mental problems as physical events. Relax the body, remove the sources of stress, and you transform your partner's outlook. After ten minutes of Super Massage chronically worried individuals often have trouble remembering what they were worried about.

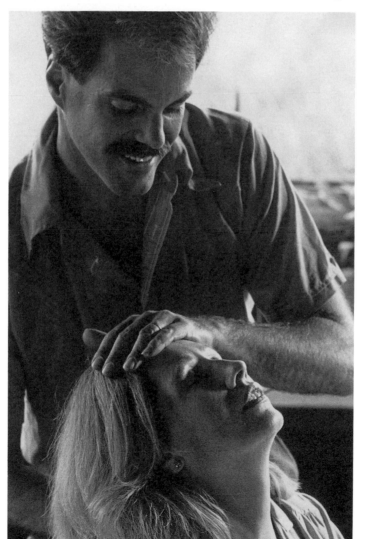

---

*"...the peculiar calm, soothing, restful, light feeling that is the most frequent result of massage cannot be understood until experienced. It doubtless arises to a great extent from the pressure of natural worn-out *debris* being speedily removed from off terminal nerve-filaments." From Graham, *A Treatise on Massage*, p. 111.

Benefits to the Skin and Hair

Massage breaks loose dead, brittle skin cells, exposing the living tissue below. When the subcutaneous tissues are super oxygenated, the skin becomes smoother, more supple.

Unfortunately for the makers of various gooey "miracle" ointments, hair is nourished only from within the scalp. Scalp massage (see p. 87) stimulates the surface blood vessels and the sebaceous glands, which will secrete various oils while you work. After four minutes of scalp massage, the hair appears glossy and moisturized.

Relaxation in Minutes

Most of the solutions that follow, for headaches, insomnia, back pain, and other ailments, require that you spend only a few minutes massaging a single part of the body. In minutes the astonishing fluid release effect begins working spectacular changes inside your partner's body (see chart). Most people you massage will probably have no idea how effective massage can be in controlling stress. You can cite scientific experiments to prove its power, you can point to recent athletic success stories, celebrity beauty treatments, or the new wave of in-house corporate massage but, ultimately, your partner must actually experience a massage to believe in it.

This book is meant to be used. See it as a tool; lay it open flat beside you while you're doing massage. Get familiar with the four basic strokes (see p. 32) but don't worry if you can't do them perfectly. Throughout the book you'll find detailed instructions for adapting each one of them to specific parts of the body. Once you've read this chapter, simply find out what's bothering your partner, turn to the appropriate chapter, and start massaging.

To be successful, the fluid release effect requires many repetitions of the "essential

strokes," which appear at the beginning of each chapter. They're easy to learn — nearly all are variations of the four basic strokes. Don't hesitate to repeat simple movements dozens, even hundreds of times each. Repetition is far more important than variety in massage.

Once you've completed the essential movements, try a few of the general strokes which are included in each chapter. There's no need to fit them all into one massage — save a few for next time. Whether you do a three-minute headache massage or a ten-minute erotic session, your stroking should be focused and consistent for the entire period.

Expect some resistance before a first massage. People take their tensions so seriously that a possible quick fix may appear frivolous. But, as every masseur knows, it happens all the time. Using your own hands and a bottle of warm oil, you can relieve stress without help from special equipment, pills, or extended treatment schedules.

Results come in five minutes, not five weeks or five months. Get started quickly and minimize conversation — the message is the massage. Finally, don't be afraid of a nervous partner. In a tense situation, the massage itself becomes an ice breaker because, as you begin, the last thing your partner expects is about to occur: pain disappears and pleasure takes its place.

After five minutes of super massage:

Acidic irritants and wastes are removed from the muscles.
Pain is controlled — the nerves are soothed.
Cramped tendons and ligaments are stretched.
Local circulation is boosted without speeding up the heart.
The oxygen content of the tissues is increased.

Which means that:

Headaches disappear without pills.
Facial wrinkles are smoothed.
Tension vanishes and relaxation takes its place.
Feelings of depression are replaced by a positive, optimistic outlook.
Digestion, circulation, skin quality, muscle tone, and sleep are enhanced.
Endurance increases.

2.
Learn
Super Massage
in One
Evening

A basic stress-control sequence

- ☛ Stroking super-oxygenates the tissues.
- ☛ Kneading squeezes wastes out of the tissues.
- ☛ Friction lubricates the joints and reaches internal organs.
- ☛ Percussion soothes the nerves and boosts circulation to a large area.
- ☛ Stroking again clears all wastes and bring in super-oxygenated blood.

When Should You Do Super Massage?

In classic full body massage your partner needs to relax the entire body before you massage any part of it. When all distractions have been removed, he will lie down on a comfortable, warm surface without clothes, jewelry, or thoughts of this world. Only then does the actual massage begin, and it can last for an hour or more. However, if long sessions with complete nudity and total relaxation become a prerequisite for every massage, your opportunities to help people will decline. Stressed individuals, in particular, will usually find a reason to avoid massage if a lengthy preparation is involved. Don't give them an out.

When your partner is suffering from a single stress-induced problem, a time-consuming full body massage may not be necessary. After just a few minutes of Super Massage directed to a single part of the body, amazing changes can occur. You may want to tell your partner that before you begin.

The continual work done by the body to support the head, arms, hands, and fingers is so fatiguing that nearby muscles are often kept in a state of tension all day long. After a while sufferers resign themselves to hours of neck, shoulder, or lower back pain every

day. As modern life becomes more automated and less physical, this low-level pain, known as background tension, is becoming a fact of life in many professions. Unfortunately, even an hour of vigorous exercise may not be enough to offset the effects of eight hours spent sitting at a desk or standing behind a counter. What, then, is the answer? Will the coffee break be replaced by an aspirin or Valium break? Must we graduate to stronger drugs to cope with increased job demands?

Enter Super Massage and the three-minute stress-reduction program.

Your first concern in preparing your partner for Super Massage should be to completely *relax the entire area that you plan to massage*. The head, for example, is a particularly heavy object that must be carried by the shoulder muscles all day long. Finding a different way to support your partner's head immediately relaxes the shoulders. Only then, as the background tension is relieved around the massage area, does truly effective neck massage become possible. The same principle applies to other supported body parts: you must take over the support before real massage can begin. Throughout the book you will find hints on how to support the head, arms, legs, and feet while you massage them.

Don't massage if:

There is an infection or fever.
There are extensive skin eruptions or bruises.
There is intense pain that shoots down a leg or interferes with sleep.
A doctor has advised against it.

Avoid massaging areas if:

Skin is bruised, cut, or erupted.
Joints are inflamed.
Veins are sensitive.
There is a tumor.
There is a painful reaction.

Quick Set-Ups at Home or at Work

Massaging on the job means compromising. You must allow for interruptions, you must work around restrictive clothes, and you must be prepared to stop in minutes when you might be tempted to go on for half an hour or more. Nevertheless, the benefits to your partner are so great that you simply cannot afford to make excessive demands. With a little ingenuity you can transform your partner's work experience and introduce massage as an aid to productivity.

It does make sense to reduce unnecessary distractions. You may want to present massage as a kind of "break" in which one takes a few minutes off from the usual demands of business. Phone calls, meetings, and appointments are simply put on hold for a few minutes. Give your partner some idea of how much time you will need. Allow him at lease a minute or two of relaxation afterward for the massage to sink in.

Don't allow your partner's anxieties to become your own. Remain calm and proceed in an orderly fashion. Remember, *continual* stress is most dangerous. Before you lay hands on your partner, it's useful to do whatever you can to break the pattern of relentless stress. Unplug the phone (or turn on the answer-

ing machine), turn off an intercom, or just close the office door. Dimming the lights makes it easier for your partner to close his eyes and drift off. The idea is to create a space in the busy day for relaxation. Then say a few words about releasing tension—give your partner "permission" to relax for a while. Don't be discouraged if your partner seems too busy for massage or actually ridicules your efforts. (See the hints for massaging stress addicts on p. 99.)

Try to simplify all preparations. If you're planning to use oil, have the squeeze bottle filled and scented. Bring your own pillow if your partner isn't likely to have one handy. Lay out towels and other accessories nearby. Don't move furniture or equipment unless it's absolutely necessary to do so.

You can do things for your partner at home that are difficult in a less intimate setting. You don't have to work around (or through) layers of clothes. Interruptions disappear, along with the usual on-the-job demands to get involved with stressful activities the moment a Super Massage is completed. Once nudity becomes possible, the full range of massage movements can be focused on every part of the body. And

afterward, while the effects of your massage soak in, your partner can relax and do absolutely nothing.

All that's needed to massage at home is a warm, quiet place large enough for the two of you. But if you're going to work with a nude partner, you do need to pay special attention to the temperature of the massage surface. A few simple preparations will make the difference between an unforgettable experience and an unpleasant one for your partner. The normal reduction in all metabolic functions that occurs when the body is at rest is accelerated during massage. In the midst of an energetic fluid release sequence, you may feel perfectly comfortable while your naked partner could be on the verge of shivering. Unless you warm the body first, massaging chilled muscles has little effect; cold muscles will remain contracted, spreading tension throughout the body. People simply cannot relax when chilled, so a cold massage surface is never acceptable.

Unless you live in the tropics, the area where you massage should be warmer than normal room temperature—at least 75 degrees Fahrenheit. The best way to insure your partner's comfort is to set up an electric heater close to the

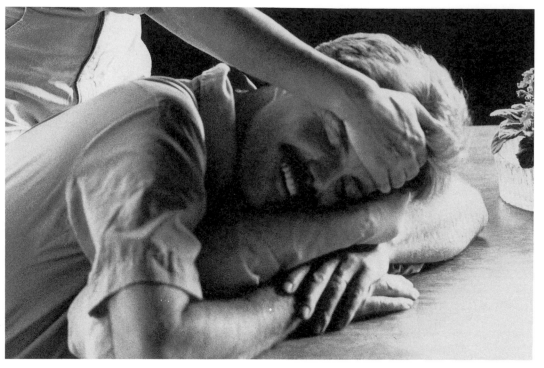

massage surface. If you're working on the floor, the room temperature will probably have to be considerably higher than usual. While any heater will do the job, an oil-filled electric radiator is best for warming a massage area. They're fast, clean, safe, and utterly silent. Most models have thermostats and wheels. While your partner takes a hot bath or shower—always a good idea before extended massage—bring the room up to a comfortable temperature.

Trust is particularly important in all massage, the more so if your partner is nude. From the moment she lies down in front of you, eyes closed and totally naked, an implicit understanding, that you are going to be very careful with her body, exists. Above all she must trust you not to do anything that would be painful. Pain has no place in massage. One ill-advised finger poke or overtwisted joint can shatter an hour of peace and relaxation. It also violates the unspoken contract between a masseur and his partner: *I will never hurt you, I will only give you pleasure.*

If it's a first massage, your partner may have no idea what to expect. Anything you can do to create a relaxed atmosphere in your massage area will help her begin to unwind and surrender to the more subtle effects. Low lights and soft music help create the right mood.

Find a firm but cushioned surface for massage, one that will permit you to press down hard on the more intense back movements without losing control. Four inches of

foam rubber is ideal; a few thick blankets covered with a sheet will do almost as well. Avoid waterbeds and very soft mattresses.

If you're working on several parts of the body, you'll need room to move around your partner during the massage. Put everything you need within reach before you begin. Hesitation (while you move a chair or search for your glasses) spoils the mood. You should remain invisible during massage so that what your partner actually experiences is purely tactile.

Finally, lay out your towels and place a bottle of heated oil near the part of the body you plan to massage first. To warm your hands, hold them tightly under your armpits for a minute or two, or cover them with a hot towel. You may want to say a few words to help with the transition between normal reality, where all the senses are used, and massage, where nearly everything that is experienced is simply felt. Something complimentary about your partner works well. If you must speak during a massage, your tone is generally more important than what is actually said.

Oiling

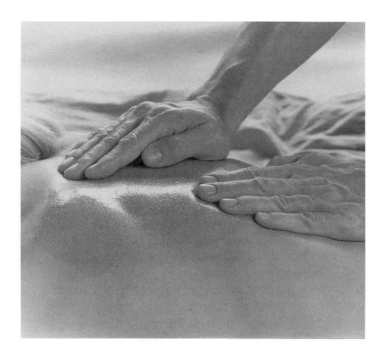

All massage strokes, except percussion and friction movements, work better if you lubricate your partner's skin first with a light vegetable oil. "Commercial" massage oils are often nothing more than ordinary vegetable oil which has been renamed, overpackaged, and overscented. You can save time and money by scenting a small bottle of ordinary coconut, sesame, or safflower oil with a few drops of fresh lemon juice. Olive, corn, and peanut oils are too thick for massage. Lemon scent is generally pleasing and has practical benefits for both the masseur and his partner. The skin's natural acidity, under daily attack from soaps (the hands are almost always the first part of the body to wrinkle), is restored by lemon juice. Many other essences and perfumes can be used — the most important consideration in choosing a scent, however, is to please your partner. Some people prefer bringing their own scent for the oil to a massage.

If you'd like to try something exotic, one commercial massage oil, called Monoi Tiare from Tahiti, stands out from all the rest. It's sultry floral scent unmistakably evokes the enchanted islands of the South Pacific. Once a rare and much sought-after prize,

this exquisite oil is now available in most parts of the United States. Check for it at your local bath shop.

You can put your oil in a simple bowl or, to avoid spills, use a plastic squeeze bottle. To please your partner the oil should be heated first. Place the container in a cup of hot water until the oil is close to body temperature. Choosing the right temperature and the right scent (for your partner) is very important because oiling often marks the beginning of a Super Massage. You oil first, then you massage. If it's your partner's first massage, remember that with oiling you're establishing the

initial contact. Avoid an impersonal, casual, or mechanistic approach. Oiling should be a deliberate part of the massage itself.

Always add oil to your own hands first, then transfer it to your partner's body. Spread the oil slowly, with even, circular movements, using the whole surface of your hands. Avoid jerky, scrubbing motions. Add just enough oil to permit your hands to move smoothly without pulling at the skin. Too much oil makes for a sloppy massage. Use extra oil carefully. Body hair requires a few additional drops; add a bit more if skin begins catching at your hands

during an extended kneading or circulation movement. Be careful not to break contact with your partner when adding oil. On the fleshier parts of the body simply turn one hand over, maintain contact with the backs of your fingers, and add oil to the upraised palm. If you must remove both hands for a moment, press a knee or the side of an arm against your partner so that some body contact is maintained.

After the massage, oil comes off easily with a light towel or with rubbing alcohol. Alcohol must be used cold, which limits its effectiveness in massage. Some people crave the exhilarating shock, others feel it shatters the calm mood you've just established.

Oiling provides a unique sensual experience that you can return to again and again during a massage. Combine it with various movements so the oiling blends with the massage or during high-volume fluid release techniques that require many repetitions of the same movement. Add more oil without breaking the rhythm. Take your time when oiling. Think about what your partner is feeling. Let your partner savor the deliciously warm scented oil as it spreads slowly across the body.

Repetition and Relaxation

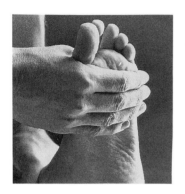 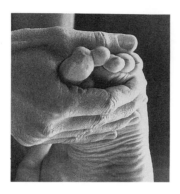 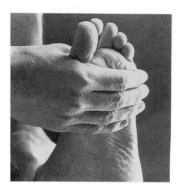 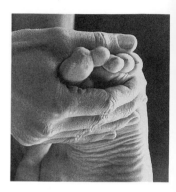

In an ordinary full-body massage most movements will be repeated three or four times. If one maintains a steady rhythm, it takes an hour or more to cover the whole body from head to foot. During a Super Massage, however, you concentrate all of your attention on a single stressed area. Rather than repeat a hundred movements three or four times, you repeat three or four movements a hundred times each. Don't be frightened by the big numbers—almost every sport routinely calls for much greater repetition. A bicyclist who pedals three or four hundred times is just warming up; so is the serious swimmer or runner after the first couple of laps. Actually, the repetition you're called upon to do during a Super Massage is much less strenuous. It doesn't require great strength

or speed, and you're not expected to compete against yesterday's score. Just relax, focus on your stroking, and keep going. You can do it easily without breathing hard.

If you're counting to yourself while stroking, remember that your partner definitely isn't. Whenever something feels good, people never count—they just want more. After the first fifty repetitions you will begin to feel tensed muscles relax under your hands as the amazing fluid release effect starts working. Add another two hundred strokes, and it will still be working the next morning.

Your stroking frequencies can vary greatly. Large-area strokes like the magnificent full body circulation movement, which takes close to a full minute to move from the feet to the head and back, simply cannot be rushed. Throughout the book, however, you will focus on the workhorse strokes of the fluid release effect, local kneading, and friction variations, which are most effective when repeated about fifty times per minute on a single spot. Again, don't be put off by the large numbers. Ordinary walking continues for hours at comparable frequencies without causing noticeable fatigue. Remember that irregular bursts of speed can destroy the hypnotic mood you're working to create. On the faster strokes, find a frequency that you can maintain easily and stay with it.

When you massage a single limb, hand, or foot, it's always best to spend some time on the other one as well. You may be working on a specific complaint that occurs on only one side of the body, say, a cramp in the left leg. The cramped area will be tight as a drum, especially when compared to the same area on the other leg. Nevertheless, after a complete fluid release sequence the cramp will probably yield, leaving the left leg so profoundly relaxed that the right leg will begin to feel tense by comparison. This is not to say that you must automatically double the amount of time spent massaging each part of the body. If you do nothing at all, the massaged limb will feel lighter and more energetic than the non-massaged one for hours, even days afterward. Just a minute or two spent on the opposite limb will add balance to your massage.

Get feedback on frequency and pressure preferences from your partner. Some people like raw speed while others prefer slower, more penetrating strokes. If it's a first massage, you may have to experiment for a few minutes while your partner sorts through the new sensations. (When she moans with pleasure you're doing something right—keep doing it.) Whatever stroke you do it's important to ask yourself, "What is my partner *feeling* right now?" You create feelings with your hands during every stroke, and those feelings are the only true measure of any massage.

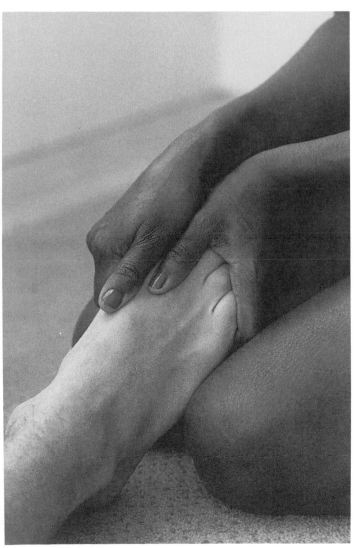

Do

Ask about painful areas before massage. Stay away from bruises and any place where the skin is broken.

Remove jewelry from the entire massage area.

Warm your hands before you start.

Use heated oil in a plastic squeeze bottle.

Create a quiet, peaceful atmosphere in the room.

Insist on no interruptions while massaging. Phone calls and appointments must wait. Children and pets should be cared for by somebody else.

Be scrupulous about your personal hygiene.

Support the entire area to be massaged with a part of your body or a pillow.

Maintain the same rhythm throughout. All strokes move at the same speed.

Keep your fingers together.

Keep all movements smooth and even—avoid abrupt transitions.

Don't

Rush or affect an ultra efficient manner. A good masseur should be invisible.

Comment on how tense your partner seems to be.

Hurt your partner. One moment of pain can ruin the entire massage.

Break contact. If you forget what to do next, continue with what you were doing.

Massage while your partner does something else.

Encourage conversation. Complaining doesn't let off steam, it usually brings on more stress. Try silence or quiet music.

Massage next to an open window on a cool day.

Compete with pain pills or tranquilizers. You will be blamed when the pills fail.

"Dig in" to soft tissues with your thumbs.

Interrupt the massage or pause between movements.

Comment on the time or wear a watch.

Four Easy-to-Learn Basic Movements: Friction

Friction is the most versatile but the most misused massage stroke. Under the right circumstances a few minutes of deep friction can reach deep inside your partner's body to provide quick relief from nagging pain. Here is a stroke that requires no oil or special preparation and can be done in almost any setting, clothed or unclothed. It's ideal for onsite stress reduction. Use it in the home, on the sports field, or at the office but not while your partner drives a car or makes a phone call. Leave that kind of friction to Hollywood.

For quick results no stroke can compete with friction because moments after you begin, the effects are registered deep within your partner's body. Friction is also a kind of natural anesthetic. Every mammal understands that rubbing a sensitive spot will bring relief. Think of friction as educated rubbing. Specialized friction movements stimulate, soothe, and warm your partner's body. Some stimulate just the skin and surface organs; others will penetrate deep within the dense tissues around joints.

Friction is easy to learn. A part of the hand, with fingers held together, ranging from the fingertips to the whole

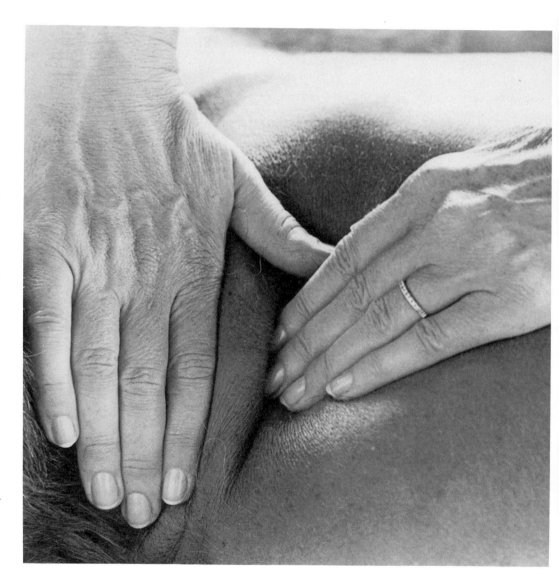

surface, is rotated against a specific spot on your partner's body. But, unlike other massage movements that glide across the surface of the body, friction will press down against the skin until you can feel the muscles within. You grip the skin while rotating your fingertips, palm, or

hand on interior muscles. Since you sometimes have to rotate fairly hard, it's easy to shake your partner's entire body during the more intense friction variations. To avoid doing this, every friction stroke must be anchored, a process that limits outward movement from the immediate massage area.

Basic Friction

Use one hand to anchor, the other to apply friction. When anchoring concentrate on what your partner will actually feel. Do you want the entire leg to flop around while you massage a knee? In order to control excessive movement while you massage, the anchor hand should press down and hold the tissues near a friction site steady. As a stroke moves, so does the anchor hand. Often the thumb is held out to control a larger area. Always anchor first, then begin friction. On fleshy parts of the body you can push a fold of flesh toward the massage site with your anchor hand, making it easier for friction to work without pulling the skin. Remember that the fingers should be held together during all friction strokes lest the deep, penetrating effects dissipate. You can sometimes feel the outline of muscles and internal organs gliding beneath your fingers.

Generally, three kinds of friction movements are used: one for thick tissues like the thighs and larger muscles; another for "hard" body areas, like the chest and feet, with large bones near the surface; and a third for the muscles of the face. Simple full hand friction for the outside of your partner's thigh will get you started with a multipurpose stroke that travels well.

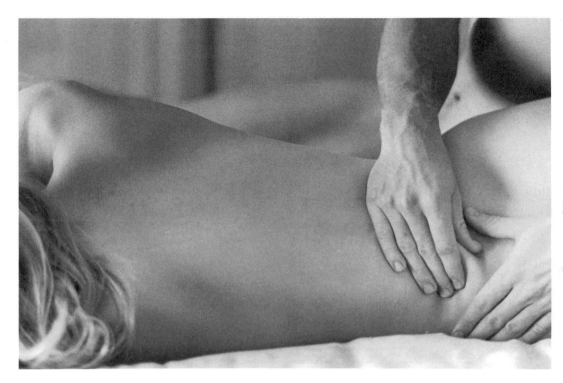

First, look for a way to anchor the stroke. If you're right-handed, open the thumb of your left hand and press down on the top of your partner's back as shown. At the same time press in toward the friction site until you are actually pushing a fold of flesh ahead of your hand. This important step relieves skin tension over the friction area. If you're left-handed, simply reverse the process. Once you've established a firm anchor, you're ready to move in with the friction hand and begin.

Use as much of the hand as possible; never "dig in" to your partner's body. Here on the back you will be able to use the whole surface of your hand from fingertips to the base of the palm. Massaging around the hands, feet, and face, you'll use just the fingertips. Press down on your partner's back, allowing your hand to bend to conform to the shape of the muscles. Use a speed that you will be comfortable maintaining for several minutes. Rotate your hand while you press. You will feel the muscles of the back rippling beneath your fingertips. Use even pressure. You may need to reposition the anchor hand from time to

time, but don't break contact with your friction hand or stop massaging to do this. Keep rotating your friction hand. You can do friction with your fingertips, the flat part of the fist, or the whole hand. Whatever method you choose, remember that interruptions are particularly distracting for your partner. Think of what she's feeling and let the feeling go on.

Kneading

If you had to settle for a single massage technique, simply learning to knead would provide a powerful tool that can be used on every part of your partner's body. Repeated kneading presses toxins out of the tissues like squeezing liquid from a sponge—it is the most important element of the fluid release effect. A thoroughly kneaded part of the body is transformed for hours, even days. Sluggish, fatigued muscles suddenly feel light and energetic, as though they had been rested overnight. The nerves are soothed and the joints work more smoothly.

Kneading is the ideal stroke to use on skeptics. Your partner doesn't have to wait to see if it works—the effects are immediate and very dramatic. In fact, a well-kneaded part of the body feels great almost from the moment you begin massage. Repeat the movement for five minutes across the bottom of a fatigued neck and you will convert almost anyone to the joys of massage.

Repetitious kneading creates a deeply hypnotic mood while it cleanses the tissues. As tension is surrendered, knotted muscles will soften under your hands, bringing forth the self-satisfied moans that every masseur knows so well. But to work properly the

kneading stroke must be consistent. Any abrupt change or hesitation will break the mood and distract your partner. Learning to control your thumbs will give you the confidence to knead a single set of muscles hundreds of times without thinking about what you're doing. Know your thumbs before you begin kneading.

Learning to knead is a two-step process: first, learn to rotate your hands in opposing circles, then add proper thumb technique. The best place to learn kneading is on the flat, fleshy outer side of your partner's thigh.

Basic Kneading

1. Start by holding your thumb flat against your forefinger and simply rotate one hand on the thigh. Keep your fingers pressed together and try to make contact with the whole surface of your hand; this may mean bending your hand slightly to conform to the shape of your partner's thigh while you circle. When you can circle effortlessly, you're ready to try it with both hands.

Do exactly the same thing with the other hand, moving in the same direction, but circle in opposition. When your first hand is at the top of a circle, your second hand will be at the bottom. Try this for a few minutes. Go ahead and lean into the stroke as you develop a gentle rhythm, using your entire arm.

2. Now add thumb technique. On every circle, simply pick up a fold of flesh with each hand between your thumb and fingers. When one thumb is wide open, the other one is picking up flesh. The thumbs are also used to direct kneading to a specific area. You can in fact focus both thumbs on the same spot. As you circle, each thumb will pick up the same fold of flesh again and again.

Once you learn how to knead, it's easy to go on for a long time almost anywhere on the body. Kneading variations include thumb and fingertip strokes for smaller parts of the body, as well as the full hand stroke shown here. As you knead you can sometimes actually feel tensed muscles soften beneath your fingertips. Keep going—what you're doing is working.

Percussion

Need a quick massage solution to on-the-job stress? Percussion movements work right through clothes and they're effective in almost any setting. A five-minute percussion break will leave your partner feeling energized, relaxed, and smiling.

If this is a first massage, your partner is probably nervous about being touched. He may be wondering how to act or what he's supposed to feel. If you're working with complete nudity, he may stiffen or start fidgeting as you begin preparing to do massage. Stress addicts (see p. 97) show fear more aggressively by arguing with you about technique, scheduling, decor, or anything else that comes to mind. Nevertheless, what most people want out of life is simply to have a good time, and that, on the most fundamental level, is exactly what massage is all about.

Ask your partner if she has ever had a full body massage. How many other experiences in life offer one uninterrupted physical pleasure for an hour or more? By saying a few words about the benefits of massage, you effectively give your partner "permission" to relax. Let the conversation end when you start massaging, because whatever you've been talking about won't seem very important after a few minutes of percussion.

Percussion (cont'd)

Percussion movements provide a good way to neutralize all kinds of elaborate defenses and get right into Super Massage. After two or three passes up and down the back, nervous conversation stops, fears evaporate, and things settle down quickly. The impact created during percussion—penetrating waves of pleasure that carry right through the whole body—is so overwhelming that most people will simply surrender to the feeling. And there's no other feeling anything like it.

Moments after you begin, things start happening fast inside the body. Deep arterial circulation is boosted, supplying the tissues with fresh oxygen and nutrients. Percussion movements reach where no other massage stroke can go. Through a combination of deep, penetrating vibration and direct pressure to various nerves, the effects of massage are transmitted to the heart, lungs, and other organs beneath the rib cage. At the same time dead skin is loosened on the surface of the body and subcutaneous muscles are toned. After a few minutes of percussion the effects sometimes become visible as your partner begins smiling to herself.

Basic Percussion

From the thickly muscled back to the delicate structures around the eyes and mouth, the amount of pressure you use will vary enormously. In most percussion strokes the contact hand—the hand that actually guides the stroke across the skin—bends to

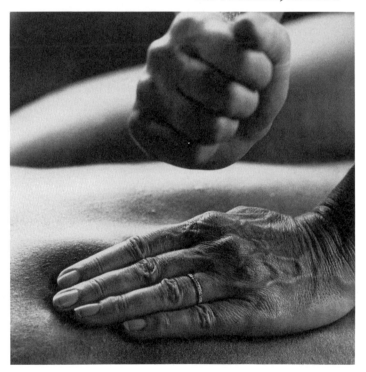

conform to the shape of your partner's body. Strike the back of the contact hand about fifty times per minute with your other hand, the percussion hand. As you strike the contact hand, slowly move it around the area you want to massage. Every "blow" must be cushioned to control pressure on

interior tissues. To regulate the force and create a more pleasing effect, the percussion hand should break at the wrist just before reaching the contact hand. Tap your partner with the side of your hand instead of pounding on her with your whole arm. Even when you apply percussion with both hands, the stroke

must still break at the wrist to be effective.

The notion that percussion movements must be painful in order to work is old and false. You don't relax tensed muscles by causing pain. In fact, pain will cause the muscles to tighten and eventually

go into spasm. *Never do anything in a massage that will hurt your partner.* One moment of pain can shatter the trust between the two of you and destroy an experience of uninterrupted pleasure.

When you're learning a percussion movement ask your partner what feels good and what doesn't. After a few dozen Super Massages you'll begin to get a sense of how much pressure different body types require. Most people want extra pressure on the heavily muscled sides of the legs and the upper back.

Percussion variations range from a vigorous pounding movement with the full hand or elbow on powerful back muscles to a tiny pinky snap, which can be used to tone delicate facial tissue. Good percussion technique, like all massage strokes, depends more on timing and control than strength or endurance. Don't rush. A steady, predictable rhythm is far more important than speed. Percussion should feel like a light rain, not a thunderstorm.

Stroking

Stroking is the easiest massage movement to learn — you'll be doing it well after a couple of tries. Some variations cover large areas of the body with a single stroke, allowing your partner the luxury of experiencing relaxation as a separate sensation that travels up a limb or across the back.

Does your partner fear relaxation on the grounds that it could undermine efficiency and drive? Are tension headaches, poor digestion, chronically aching muscles, or recurring rashes already a fact of life? Are you anxious to help but wondering where to start? Here's how to provide fast relief from the condition that seems to precede most other stress-induced problems. Stroking is the first step in reversing the dangerous pressures on the circulatory and nervous systems created by the vasoconstriction effect. With just a few dozen repetitions you can cut through stress by flooding congested tissues with fresh oxygen and nutrients.

During stroking movements you take over part of the work that is usually done by your partner's heart. After just one minute of stroking, blood circulation is significantly accelerated — your partner experiences a warm rush

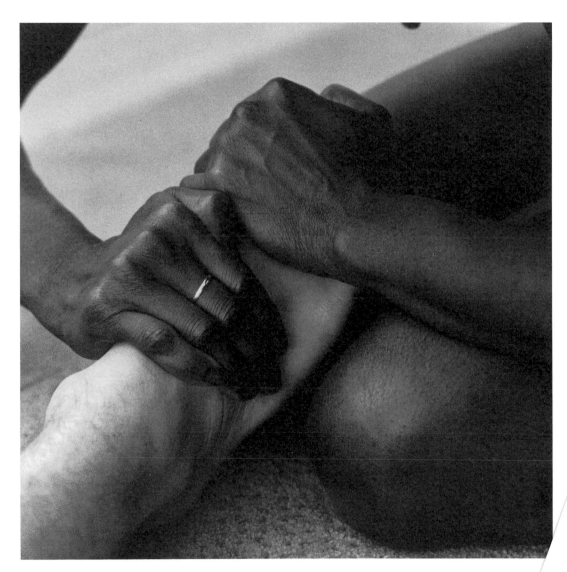

spreading outward from your hands. A stroking variation is particularly effective on the limbs, where high stress levels plus constant muscle tension tend to cut off proper blood flow. Use it on desk-

bound people to begin and end a Super Massage. Starting on the feet and ending at the waist, you can warm the entire leg as though your partner were exercising hard. Actually, he's completely relaxed and the heart rate is lower than usual.

Basic Stroking

Work toward the heart in a stroking movements. Pre down with the whole flat face of your hands as yo move up toward the he Some stroking mover that begin on the low of the body will ext the heart all the wa

Stroking (cont'd)

shoulders. Moving away from the heart, on the return part of the movement, light contact is sufficient. As you push forward with the full flat surface of your hands, hundreds of tiny intravenous valves are forced open, causing blood pressure in the major veins to decrease. Blood is then sucked into the temporary vacuum from the arteries and fresh oxygen floods the tissues. The blood pressure and heart rate decrease while circulation through the tissues is speeded up. This is the beginning of the fluid release effect that is unique to massage (see p. 17). With it you can begin to reverse the effects of accumulated tension and stress in a few minutes.

Stroking variations include back pressing, compression, and full body stroking. Generally, your fingers should be kept together when doing massage, but during stroking it's particularly important to make as much contact as possible. As your partner develops the exquisite sensual awareness that comes with repeated massage he will immediately notice the difference if your fingers drift apart — a smooth, sinuous movement becomes suddenly jagged and dissonant.

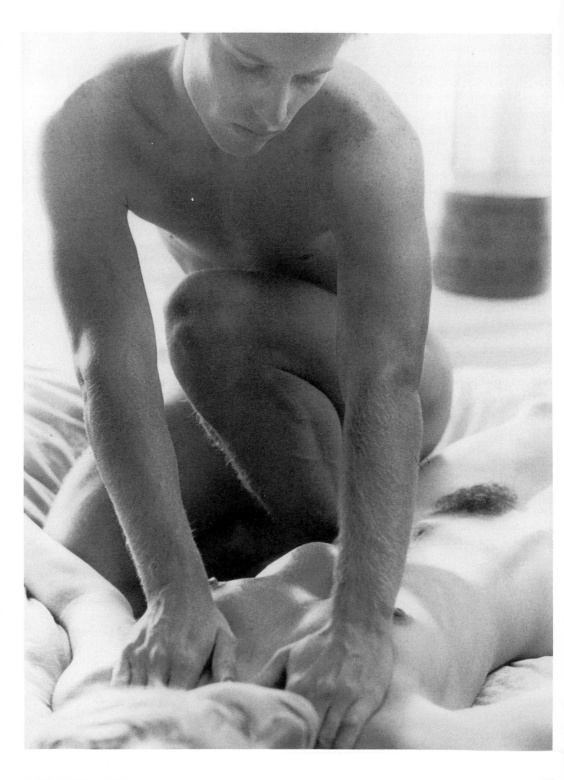

Basic Stress Control

Since every individual's body reacts differently to stress, each chapter offers several approaches to relaxing tension. One stiff neck may respond to a combination of kneading, friction, and stroking, while another will simply require a single percussion stroke repeated for several minutes. However, masseurs prefer certain movements for specific parts of the body, and these are indicated in the "essential strokes" charts at the beginning of each chapter.

Choose these strokes to create a basic but effective stress-relief sequence, and as you learn more about your partner's special needs, use the general strokes in each chapter to extend the massage. One minute spent repeating each of the movements shown on the Basic Stress-Control Sequence chart will give you a powerful five-minute massage. Shorten each of the strokes or skip the final stroking repetition when doing three- and four-minute massages.

If you have the privacy and the time, find a comfortable, warm place and massage your partner in the nude. If not, use oil where you can and give special emphasis to the percussion and friction movements that work right through clothes in virtually any setting.

If your partner is suffering from a localized problem like a headache or neck and shoulder pain, it's not necessary to read the entire book — just turn to the appropriate section and start massaging. Don't worry if your technique isn't perfect at first. Your partner will enjoy being touched and you can learn as you go.

3.
Three-Minute Relief from Headaches

Three essential strokes
One minute each, fifty repetitions

☛ Brain circulation
☛ Kneading the neck and shoulders
☛ Deep friction

What Causes Headaches?

The brain itself feels nothing: it simply registers feelings that originate elsewhere. But the entire organ is supplied by tiny blood vessels, many less than a thirty-second of an inch in diameter, which are exquisitely sensitive to mood changes. Under stress they contract sharply (the effect is even more pronounced here than elsewhere in the body), cutting back the vital oxygen supply to interior tissues. Nasty things begin to happen near the surface of the skull when the brain is starved for oxygen.

The first sign of tension within is usually transmitted directly to the face via large nerves from the center of the brain. Tiny muscles of expression are immediately pulled taut, turning smiles into grimaces. As smiling becomes a chore, tenacious little wrinkles begin to appear out of nowhere at the corners of the eyes and mouth. The jaws tighten from just below the ears and the mouth begins to feel dry. Tension spreads rapidly to the muscles of the neck and upper back. The head begins to turn awkwardly, the shoulders appear hunched, and finally the spine itself is twisted out of shape. Eventually the chin tilts forward and the posture of the head, even the whole body, is affected. With no

relief, major muscles of the neck and back, strong enough to bend the spine, clamp down on the blood vessels that supply the brain. This, of course, is the classic vicious circle of vasoconstriction; decreased circulation creates muscle tension which in turn further inhibits circulation. If nothing is done to relieve the pressure, the body will finally try to slow things down by sending an unmistakable message: a nasty headache.

Once a headache begins, it's difficult to think clearly about where it came from. Perfectly calm individuals can suffer for no apparent reason and, of course, shattering migraines, caused, perhaps, by chemical imbalances deep within the brain, can wreck an entire day. Exceptional headaches which require specialized medical attention may have little to do with muscle tension or circulation. Nevertheless, the garden variety blinding headache with shooting pain behind the eyes and a stiff neck is probably brought on by too much stress. And since the worst headaches can be so intense, panic and opiate gulping takes over at the first sign of pain. Once the more stupefying antiheadache drugs become part of the picture, massage has little chance. After a while, it simply hurts whenever you're not taking a pill.

Every masseur who knows where to look for the real source of a headache has seen throbbing pain vanish with just a few minutes of directed friction and kneading. The strokes that follow offer a drug-free method of headache control that works in minutes.

Do

Be sure the head and torso are supported.
Include the whole upper back in your massage.
Be sure your partner's eyes are closed.
Warm your hands first.

Don't

Massage while your partner does something else.
"Dig in" under the vertebrae and bony parts of the shoulders.
Put pressure directly on the spine.
Massage under a bright overhead light.

The Massage Solution

If you can reverse the vaso-constriction effect at its source, many stress-induced headaches will disappear as quickly as they appeared. Masseurs seek to release afflicted nerves and blood vessels from the iron grip of overtensed muscles. Relaxing the muscles allows constricted blood vessels to open up and permits large quantities of oxygen to be pumped directly into the brain. The question is: which tensed muscles do you relax?

Facial massage, by itself (see p. 85), is not generally effective against headaches. Only if throbbing frontal headaches centered just behind the eyes have been torturing your partner should you focus the massage on the face itself. Complete instructions are included in Chapter 7. In fact, many headaches are caused by tension in the most unlikely parts of the body. If your partner wonders exactly what you're doing under his shoulder blades or at the base of the jaw, simply ask him to repeat the question in three minutes. In just three minutes, working from the base of the neck, you can triple the oxygen content of the brain. In another minute or two, you can further relieve pressures on certain crucial nerves in the upper back until

Do these vertebrae bend easily?

local muscle tension completely vanishes. This not only gets rid of your partner's headache, it completely transforms a bad mood.

Nothing like oxygen for an irritable brain.

A Simple Tension Test

Generally, men and women experience tension in different parts of the body. Men usually complain of tightness and pain in the lower back, while women are annoyed by pervasive tension in the neck and shoulders.

Ideally, while you're stroking, your partner will simply surrender to the pleasure of massage. But if the muscles are near spasm, any kind of relaxation becomes virtually impossible. Remember: *never comment on how tense your partner seems to be*—that only

makes things worse. Watch for the nonverbal cues that indicate exactly where tension originates. On this part of the body pay close attention to the way your partner's head is carried. The head is a heavy object that must be supported all day long by the muscles of the upper back and neck. If those muscles are near spasm, your partner will find it difficult to allow her head to relax. Use this test: does the head fall back when you lift the neck? If your partner "helps" you by lifting the entire head when you raise the neck, you've located tension around the neck and shoulders. Work on the neck and shoulders for a few minutes until you feel tightened muscles begin to soften.

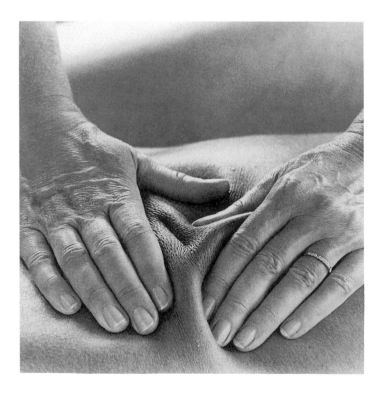

Quick headache relief
- ☛ Oxygenate the brain.
- ☛ Lift and knead the neck.
- ☛ Press the forehead for a full minute.
- ☛ Liberate the shoulder blades.
- ☛ Percussion for the heart and lungs.
- ☛ Deep friction along the spine.
- ☛ Compression.
- ☛ Elbow pounding.

Lifting the Neck

An effective neck lift allows the head to fall back in a graceful arc, reversing some of the pressures at the top of the spine. More importantly, as you lift, the muscles of the upper back are no longer required to support a heavy object that tends to lean slightly forward most of the day — your partner's head. Suddenly it falls back luxuriously beneath your hands, providing welcome relief to the whole upper back, flexing the neck, and opening all the vertebrae within. A well-executed neck lift feels as liberating as it looks.

Be sure you're well balanced and comfortable before trying any lift. Again, if your partner's eyes are open, she's not completely relaxed. Begin by cupping one hand across her eyes while pressing the fingertips of your other hand against the center of her forehead, one of the most sensitive parts of the body. Holding both hands in position for ten seconds permits your partner to close her eyes and concentrate on pure sensation. After your silent count to ten you may want to continue for a moment or two and say a few reassuring words: it's OK for her to keep her eyes closed; darkness makes the experience even more enjoyable.

When her eyes remain closed and her breathing becomes more regular, you're both ready for the lift. Clasp your fingers basket style (as shown) just beneath your partner's neck and lift straight up. Be careful not to press inward against the large blood vessels on the sides of the neck. The real pressure in this stroke should be right across your fingertips. Lift until you feel resistance, then hold your partner's neck up at the point of tension for a silent count of five before lowering it. Don't force the neck; some will bend further than others. When your partner's head falls all the way back *without resistance,* her whole upper body is close to true relaxation. Once the lift begins,

your partner is likely to ask for more, so be ready to continue for a while. Lift and lower the neck at the same speed, avoiding sudden, jerky movements. Maintain the same even rhythm with each lift.

Boosting Circulation in the Brain

With this simple circulation stroke you can begin to counter the effects of vaso-constriction inside the brain. During each stroke you're in close contact with the blood vessels that supply the brain. And each stroke pushes blood into the head, increasing both the circulation rate and blood volume, *without speeding up the heart.* Here again, there is no other way to do this outside of massage.

Before you begin oiling, move your partner's hair out of the way so the movement can be easily extended to the neck. Most upper back strokes work as well on the back of the neck. Cup your hands slightly to avoid putting direct pressure on your partner's spine. Otherwise, make contact with the full surface of both hands, from finger-tips to the base of the palm, throughout. Use moderate pressure.

The stroke begins at the center of the back, on both sides of the spine, and continues up to the base of the skull. Stay off the spine itself. Hold your hands flat, finger-tips facing up. Push up to the neck with one hand while your other hand remains in place. Apply pressure with the hand that's moving up the spine — the other hand should simply rest in place. Be ready to add extra oil if the skin soaks up the first few drops you use. At the top of the stroke allow your fingers to form themselves to the shape of your partner's shoulders. As one hand is lifted at the top of the neck, immediately begin moving up with the other so that what your partner feels is a single, smooth, uninterrupted motion — as regular as a heartbeat.

The complete stroke starts at the middle of the back, travels to the shoulder tops, then returns to the starting point. After the second or third repetition, increase the speed (but not the pressure). In a half a minute you can be moving two or three times faster than your starting rate. Now you're aiming directly for the head with a variation, called "fast stroking," which simply allows you to concentrate on increasing the blood volume in a selected part of the body.

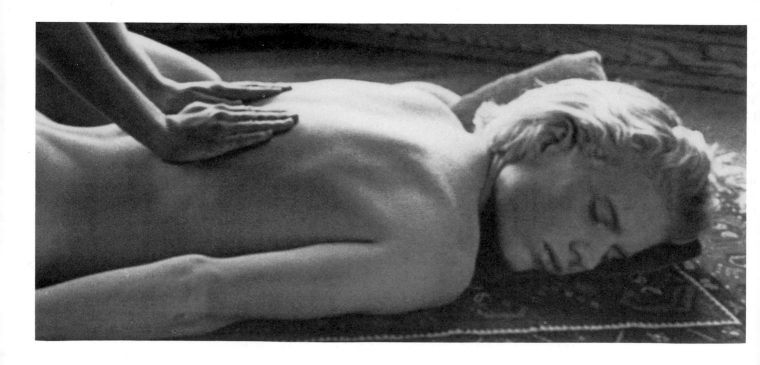

Fingertip Kneading the Neck and Shoulders

Extending from shoulder to shoulder and up onto the neck, the massive trapezius muscle dominates the upper back. Relax it in stages with a kneading stroke that can be done with the fingertips on the neck or using the whole hand on the fleshy parts of the upper back.

Remember that correct use of the thumb is always the key to effective kneading. On the upper back and neck, whether the whole hand is used or just the fingertips, each thumb must pick up a fold of flesh every time you knead.

You only need to do this stroke from one side of the body. Get comfortable next to your partner's upper arm and begin kneading one shoulder, moving across the top of the back to the opposite shoulder. Your partner should be facing you if you plan to extend your kneading to the neck itself. If he's facing away from you the possibilities for neck massage are limited because exposed blood vessels on the side of the neck make kneading difficult.

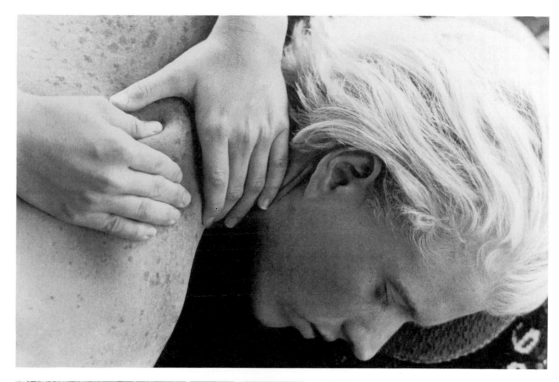

Start kneading at thirty strokes a minute (a complete stroke every two seconds). Then keep going for a full minute or more. Extended kneading is the ideal stroke for fatigued muscles.

Liberating the Shoulder Blades

As tension spreads downward from the head, major muscle groups of the upper back begin to freeze. Just as muscle tension in the neck limits the mobility of the head, tension across the top of the back begins to affect the entire upper torso. Once the back tightens up, the neck and head become even more tense. This is a typical headache syndrome, with tension from the back and head reinforcing each other. Some of the most intense headaches are caused by pressure to large nerves just below the shoulder. Look carefully at your partner's shoulders. Do they seem tight, hunched forward, or permanently elevated? Do they move freely or are they frozen in a single position?

Get comfortable next to your partner's shoulder and use this simple, very satisfying, two-step process for liberating the shoulders. First, try a series of fingertip kneading strokes from the neck down onto the center of the upper back. Then, once the muscles have been relaxed, rotate the massive bony framework of the shoulders. When you do all the work in moving your partner's body, the stroke becomes a "passive exercise." Repeated many times at a constant frequency, this kneading-rotating combination will melt the large trapezius muscle and relax the entire upper back.

Rotating the Scapula

The large, visible scapula that stands out from the back moves independently from the rib cage. By anchoring just below the rounded top of the arm with one hand and pressing down from above with the other (as shown), you can lift and turn the whole scapula. Lift from a low angle. Initially, the range of rotation will depend on just how tight your partner is feeling. Rotate slowly, keeping a firm grip on both surfaces. You'll feel an irregular sort of circle begin to emerge as you turn. Work just inside the point where you feel tension. Gradually, as you turn, the circle will become wider.

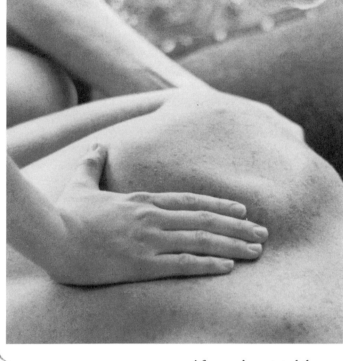

After you've rotated the scapula a half dozen times in each direction, lift it straight up with your bottom hand and apply friction under the bony protrusion with the thumb side of your top hand. Press in under the bone and let your hand follow the shape of the depression. When you're through, lower the shoulder slowly. Remember: *every motion, no matter how insignificant, is felt and becomes a part of your massage.* Make each one count.

Compression

Is your partner's headache accompanied by a stiff neck? Pressure on nerves that begin in the middle of the back may be the cause of both problems. Start by relaxing the upper back, and the neck pain will often disappear along with the headache. Compression strokes, useful on any fleshy part of the body, work best over thicker muscles, where you can bear down as the hands are rotated. This is a particularly easy movement to learn because, as the stroke travels, the initial hand-over-hand position remains the same.

Oil the entire area you plan to massage, then, with your fingers held together, press down with one hand over the other (as shown). Keep your fingers together and make certain that your bottom hand maintains full contact from the fingertips to the base of the palm throughout the movement. Begin a series of tight circles that will slowly move back and forth across the massage area. Let your fingertips bend over the shoulders and around the sides of your partner's body. After plenty of repetition, compression strokes begin to spread a warm, penetrating feeling that is so pleasant, your partner may not want you to stop.

Deep Friction

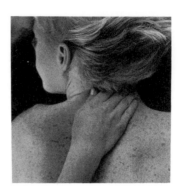

The spinal nerves link the brain with every part of the body. Vertical rows of muscles that hold the spine erect are the first to pick up tension when the nerves are irritated. Soothe those muscles and you reach deep within the spine to the body's major nerves. A more direct connection to the brain cannot be found anywhere in the body.

Locate the ridge of raised muscles that run parallel to each side of the spine. On the lower back these muscles can actually pull the spine slightly out of alignment, causing truly alarming pain. At the top of the back, thick, bony structures keep things in place, but excessively tense muscles next to the spine can still cause terrible discomfort.

This is the source of several remote problems, most commonly stiff necks and headaches.

Anchor your friction movement above or below your working hand. This stroke will take you very close to the spine, but you should avoid pressing directly on sensitive vertebrae. Push down with the fingertips of your friction hand and circle on the muscles. Move up and down the side of the spine from mid-back (not below the bottom ribs) to the base of the neck. Spend extra time on the back of the neck—five strokes for every one you did near the spine. Much of the tension you felt along the spine has been concentrated here. Anchor against the front of your partner's forehead. Feel for the thick neck muscles and rotate your hands on the hardest spots. Again, avoid pressing on the spine itself.

Elbow Pounding

Is your partner beset by minor aches and pains? Here is a way to make something powerful and very pleasant happen that may release him from his worries. With elbow pounding you can sometimes completely replace low-level irritations and nagging pains with the overwhelming feeling of the stroke itself. At the very least, this movement will relax the large muscles of the middle back, the hidden source of many headaches. Don't try to resist elbow pounding; the effects are immediate and overpowering. Intense vibrations spread from the point of contact and can carry right through your partner's body. No massage stroke uses more pressure and no stroke penetrates more deeply. Even so, one doesn't simply pound away with complete abandon. The stroke works best if it's carefully controlled so that the percussion effect can be aimed effectively.

During elbow pounding, as in all percussion movements, (see page 35), the actual "blow" is cushioned by part of your own body. Here, you simply place your elbow against the muscle, bend the hand back, and pound against the base of the palm with the other hand (as shown). Find the two muscu-

lar ridges that run parallel to the spine. If your partner is suffering from a headache, most likely at least one of the ridges will be raised and obviously tight. During the stroke, let your elbow ride along each ridge from the midback, just above the bottom of the rib cage, all the way up to the base of the neck. Stay off the neck itself. This is a powerful stroke— don't overdo it. Avoid "digging in" to the muscles with your elbow. Again, ride along the surface, letting the elbow push into the muscle only at the moment of the blow. Half of your arm absorbs the blow so what your partner actually feels is a generous vibration that begins near the spine and penetrates deep within. Here on the upper back, elbow pounding travels well as long as you confine it to major muscles and avoid the spine itself. Make at least three complete passes over each area you pound.

4.
Three-Minute Relief from Neck and Shoulder Pain

Three essential strokes
One minute each, fifty repetitions

☛ Circulation (stroking)
☛ Fingertip kneading
☛ Deep friction

Relaxing the Neck and Shoulders

Neck and shoulder pain, once practically the exclusive complaint of women, now shows up nearly as often in men. When dealing with work-related stress, many of the serious neck and shoulder problems you will encounter will come from people who operate typewriters and computers. Since a woman's shoulder muscles are often disproportionately smaller than a man's, the effort of supporting the head, a heavy object, for hours in the fixed positions required by office work can generate severe tensions. However, computer work is so demanding on the neck and shoulder muscles of *any* operator that, eventually, certain aches and pains are simply taken for granted.

Away from the office, we experiment with various exercises and drugs, and when they fail, resign ourselves to perpetually tense shoulders and aching necks. Constant stress then takes its inevitable toll; bad moods last longer, irritable behavior becomes the rule, and, eventually, major personality changes are established.

The massage solution to aches and pains in the neck and shoulders calls for many repetitions of a few simple movements. A single fingertip kneading stroke, for example, can easily be repeated more than one hundred times in only three minutes. Whether your partner is male or female, you can begin to change fixed patterns of tension in the neck and shoulders with your first Super Massage.

Rotating and Pulling the Head

Does your partner have a noisy neck? When the head is turned from side to side do you sometimes hear grinding or popping sounds? Interior stiffness almost anywhere in the body can eventually lead to the kind of chronic aches that make it impossible to escape from pain. Use the following movement—a simple passive exercise—to restore the natural mobility of the neck. It will stretch out stiff ligaments, flex the cervical vertebrae, and leave your partner smiling.

When rotating and pulling various parts of the body, you will find natural "handles" just about everywhere you want them to be. The head, for example, can be grasped at the base of the skull and beneath the chin (as shown). Supported at both points, it rotates evenly.

Slowly turn your partner's chin toward one shoulder until you feel resistance, then stop—the moment you reach the point of tension, it's time to begin rotation. There's no need to lift the head more than an inch or two. Simply pull straight back under the chin and the base of the skull, then turn the head slowly

from one shoulder to the other. A flexible neck permits the head to turn almost all the way across, but, of course, stiffness will limit the arc. Never force the head past the point of tension, and try not to call attention to tensed muscles. Super Massage, not talk, will loosen the stiffness. At the far side of each rotation, pause for a moment, then bring your partner's head back to the starting point. Keep the arc smooth and even. During this move-

ment it is particularly important to avoid short, jerky motions. After ten rotations, the point of tension begins to recede gradually as the neck becomes more supple.

Circulation for the Upper Back

Start relaxing the neck and shoulders from far below. Two clearly visible vertical ridges of muscles run parallel to each side of the spine, helping to hold it in place. Trace these muscles with a series of long circulation strokes that will turn across the shoulders and descend to a starting point just above the beginning of the rib cage.

Sit comfortably near your partner's waist. Some people appreciate a small pillow under the head and beneath the ankles. Begin by pressing the base of your palms against the muscles near the middle of the back (as shown). With your hands in place press all of your fingers forward until they lay flat on either side of the spine. If your hands are significantly wider than the spinal muscles, let your fingers ride on the outside of the muscles. Never press directly on the spine itself.

As you push up along the spine, distribute pressures equally from the base of the palms to your fingertips.

Turn at the base of the neck and move out to the shoulders, letting your fingers mold themselves to the contour of your partner's body. Turn again at the outside of the shoulders and begin your descent along the sides of the back, fingers pointing toward the massage surface. Turn a final time at the middle of the back and return to the starting position. Practice this stroke a few times until the various turns flow into each other and the entire stroke becomes a single, smooth, uninterrupted movement.

What your partner feels is a wave of sensation flowing up the center of the back and down his sides. Usually, by the fourth or fifth repetition you will feel the spinal muscles begin to soften. If they're still tense, continue, even if it means extending the entire massage session, until you feel a change. Your partner will appreciate the extra consideration.

Fingertip Kneading the Spine

Whether you're massaging around the top or bottom of the back, it's crucial to relax the long muscles that run parallel to the spine. Any pressure on the spine itself will create tension throughout the whole neck and shoulder area. This basic fingertip kneading stroke travels so well that you can find ways to use it on nearly every part of the body. It's especially good on hard-to-reach spots where full hand kneading becomes difficult.

This stroke moves exactly the same way as full hand kneading but the contact is more specific. Grasping a small fold of flesh with your fingertips permits you to direct the kneading effect to a single set of muscles, while excluding the surrounding tissue. The spinal muscles, for example, can be kneaded with your fingertips while the spine and rib cage remain unaffected.

Get comfortable and reach across to the opposite side of your partner's spine. You can knead both sides of the spine without changing position. While moving the hands in opposing circles, pick up a fold of flesh between the fingers and thumb of one hand while the other hand is open wide (as shown). As you move up and down the spinal muscles, first one hand then the other will pick up a fold of flesh. Begin fingertip kneading just above the bottom of the rib cage and move up toward the neck along the long muscles that run parallel to the spine. Knead the side

of the neck and the shoulders before moving back down the same side of the spine. Massage one side of the spine at least three times, then do the other. After a few repetitions you can often feel tension melt as the spinal muscles become relaxed and supple.

Real relaxation for the neck and shoulders is now within reach.

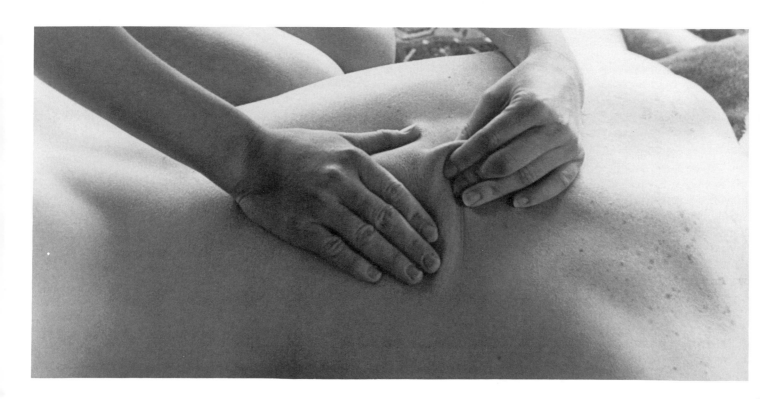

Deep Friction

Happily, neck and shoulder fatigue can disappear remarkably fast. Even after days of discomfort, headaches and assorted aches and pains will vanish in minutes with the right massage treatment. Most fatigued backs long for several minutes of uninterrupted deep friction. Here is a way to extend the friction strokes from the headache chapter to include the whole of the upper back. When spreading friction across the upper back, stay off the spine, shoulder blades, and bony shoulder tops. Large, powerful muscles of the upper back will accept pressure from the whole surface of your hand (from the fingertips to the base of the palm). Deep friction strokes on this part of the body require more pressure than most massage movements. Be sure your partner is comfortable and well cushioned.

Kneel or sit cross-legged on a small pillow below your partner's shoulder. Give equal attention to both sides of the spine during upper-back friction strokes. If your partner's neck is so stiff that the head doesn't turn easily, you may want to support the shoulders from below with a couple of small pillows.

Anchor the stroke above or below the massage area, using the whole surface of one hand. Keep the thumb and forefinger spread wide for best control. When repositioning of the anchor hand becomes awkward, keep it in place and press under it with your friction hand. Open the thumb and forefinger (as shown) and push a fold of flesh under the forefinger with your friction hand. Locate the muscles you want to massage with the fingertips of your friction hand, then lower your whole hand onto your partner's body. With your fingers pressed together, push down and rotate on the muscular tissue below. Let your hand form itself to the changing shape of your partner's body as the stroke travels from one part of the back to another. Do one side of the spine thoroughly, then the other.

Pounding

The Forearm Press

If your partner moans and groans with pleasure throughout a friction movement, you can intensify the feeling, without changing your position, with pounding, a delightful percussion variation. Vibrations from this stroke will penetrate deep within, in some cases *right through* your partner's body. Percussion strokes have a way of taking over and creating a reality of their own. Let it happen.

Provide a cushion for your pounding stroke by striking the back of one hand with the other. It's best to pound on the back of the fingers (as shown) and let the vibration carry through to your partner's body. Move the contact hand, as you pound, to focus the stroke on the heavily muscled parts of the upper back. Again, stay off the spine itself, and the neck.

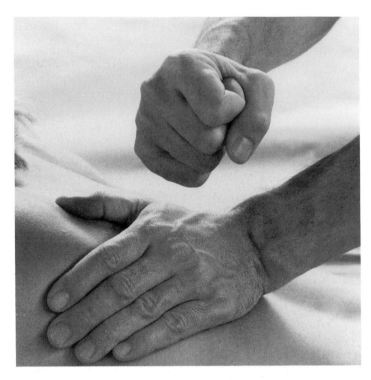

Remember that the key to effective percussion is restraint; all the "blows" should be cushioned and carefully directed. You want a light rain, not a thunderstorm.

One simple rule in massage is to do big things on the big parts of the body and save the little things for little parts of the body.

Since the back is the very largest part of the body, it fairly cries out for a luxurious stroke like the forearm press. The moment you begin, your partner feels a languid warmth spreading slowly across the whole upper torso; just right after deep, penetrating friction sequences.

The forearm press is easier to do if you reach across your partner's spine and massage the opposite side of his back. Keep the flat part of your clenched fist down and in contact at all times. The two main points of contact are on the flat part of the knuckles and against the fleshy inner forearm. On curved parts of the body, such as the sides, bend your knuckles and keep the forearm down on the flat part of the back as you rotate. Generally, the whole forearm and hand will rotate as one. As the forearm press moves up and down the back, lean into it to avoid breaking contact at any point.

Circling slowly with your contact hand, covering the back from the bottom of the rib cage to the shoulders, continue up and down the back at the same speed for a full minute or two.

Compression

If your partner has a stiff neck *and* seems nervous, try several minutes of compression on the upper back. Compression strokes are one of the quickest antidotes to nervous tension. (More on that in Chapter 8.) They are easy to do and will work with little preparation in almost any setting. The penetrating, immensely soothing motion has a hypnotic effect that calms jangled nerves.

Effective almost anywhere on the body, compression movements are especially useful on the fleshy parts of the back. Simply place one open hand on top of the other, press down, and rotate in small circles. As you rotate, let your fingers curl around the edges of your partner's body, maintaining full contact from the fingertips to the base of the palm. Large muscle groups will accept plenty of pressure — check with your partner to see what feels good. Intense movements, like compression and friction, must stay off bony protrusions around the spine and shoulder blades, and avoid the sides of the neck. Cover the whole fleshy surface on one side of the spine with compression, then do the other side. Repeat the movement at least three times.

Rolling

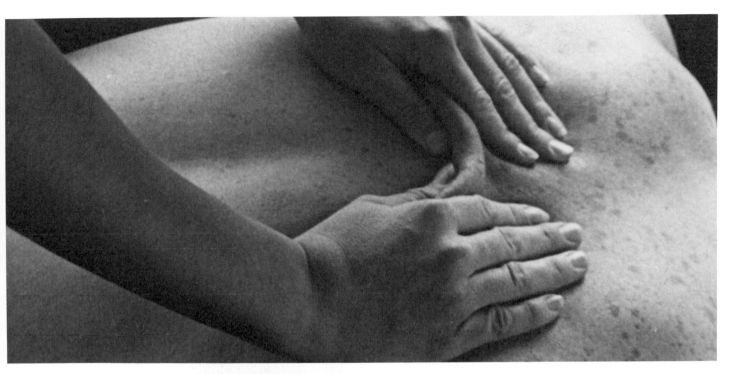

Here is a pleasing variation of the popular fingertip kneading stroke. Rolling allows you to amplify the plucking part of kneading during which the thumb and forefinger grasp a tiny fold of flesh. Typically, when you are fingertip kneading the upper back, only the tips of the fingers can be used to pick up flesh, but with this variation you can fold the flesh over the

whole length of your forefingers. It's sometimes surprising just how large an area you can roll. Even on well-muscled backs, your forefingers will disappear beneath the long fold of flesh.

Put your hands down on your partner's back palm side down. Move in to the area you want to roll until your fingertips are nearly facing each other on opposite sides of the spine. Push down with your fingers until a small fold

of flesh appears above your thumbs. Then use your thumbs to fold it back over the forefingers (as shown). Once you've grasped the fold of flesh, push forward with both forefingers while pulling back with the thumbs. You're ready to roll — use both thumbs at once.

5.
Three-Minute Relief from Lower Back Pain

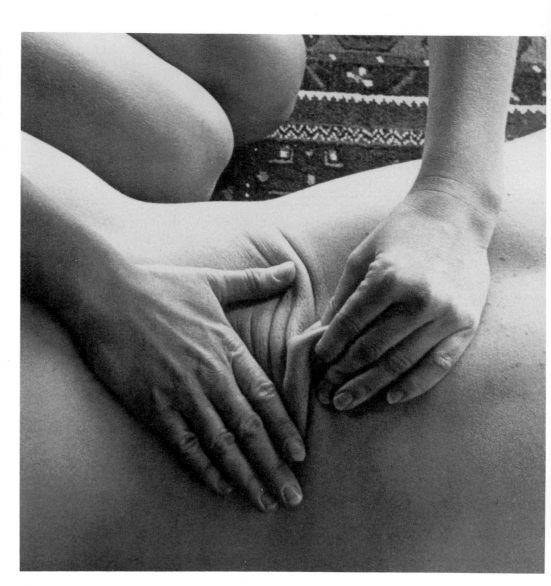

Three essential strokes
One minute each, fifty repetitions
- ☛ Back stretching
- ☛ Kneading the side of the back
- ☛ Hip friction

How to Avoid Lower Back Pain

This part of the book is mainly (but not exclusively) for men. In Chapter 3 we saw how women tend to experience tension in the neck and shoulders — men are most sensitive around the lower back. Sudden cramps next to the spine can bend the whole body to one side, making standing up a painful ordeal. Panic takes over quickly — how do you adjust to pain that doubles you over? This close to the spine, however, immobilizing pain can be caused by nothing more serious than a local muscle spasm. Nevertheless, to be certain there's no structural damage, whenever severe pain occurs in the lower back, your partner should be checked by a doctor before beginning massage.

Most lower back pain arrives so suddenly and is so intense that your partner may fear the worst: the dreaded slipped disc. But powerful back

muscles pulling hard on the bottom of the spine can cause almost as much discomfort without doing any permanent damage. The moment the spine is bent past a certain point, intense pressure builds on the nerves of the lower back. Pain so excruciating that your partner may have difficulty standing up straight can follow. If the source of the pain is muscular (most lower back complaints are), use Super Massage to straighten up the back in just three minutes.

Look carefully at the muscles of your partner's back. Don't be intimidated by a rock-hard ridge on one side of the spine — you've probably found the problem. The tension will yield, gradually, to a combination of passive exercise and massage. When cramped muscles contract so fiercely that they refuse to expand, the immediate problem is lack of oxygen. However, before you can oxygenate the tissues, it's important to begin as you would with any cramped muscles: stretch out the whole lower back.

Quick Relief from Cramps: Back Stretching

Kneading the Side of the Back and the Buttocks

Back stretching is Super Massage at its very best. By providing fast, drugless pain relief, this single movement can eliminate hours, days, or even weeks of suffering. Since most lower back cramps are stress induced, the initial muscle spasm has a nasty habit of striking at the most inconvenient times: just before a board meeting, during a tense negotiation, or while packing for a much needed holiday. Happily, back stretching requires no special preparation or equipment. In the office, at home, or at play—wherever pain strikes—you will be ready to help.

Whenever you're working on a cramp, be gentle—forcing the issue will cause more pain. Pull down on the cramped lower back muscles by pressing your partner's knees against her chest. This simple movement has a curious side effect: as the muscles on the backs of the legs are pulled tight, the long muscles that run parallel to the spine are stretched out.

Support your partner's legs with both hands as you lift until her knees are straight up. Then flex the knees and press forward on her shins with the fleshy part of your forearm (as shown). It's important to move slowly and deliberately throughout this

sequence. Avoid sudden, jerky movements when you lift, press, and lower the leg. An unhurried, consistent rhythm works best. Press to the point of tension, hold for a silent count of ten, then lower the legs to the starting position. Remember: as you press down on the knees, you're stretching out cramped muscles in the lower back. If you're not sure where to stop, get some feedback from your partner. (Moaning and smiling means you've got it just right—keep going.) As the muscles of the lower back begin to relax, the point of tension will gradually recede. Release your partner from the cramp, and the pain will vanish as quickly as it appeared. Repeat the movement at least three times.

A perennial favorite of masseurs, the side and the buttocks offer the best opportunity for kneading anywhere in the body. Most kneading strokes must work around bony structures or stay within a single small area. On the buttocks, however, you're finally free of bony obstacles and major surface blood vessels, so there's no reason to limit the stroke to your fingertips. Reach across your partner's body, open up your hands on the side, and knead.

The large gluteal muscles in the buttocks receive almost no benefit from ordinary walking or running; you have to actually climb something before the muscles begin to tighten. Thus, the alarming pear-shaped figure that mysteriously plagues so many committed runners. To be sure, your partner may have significant cosmetic reasons for toning the buttocks, but for highly stressed individuals who live on the threshold of excruciating back cramps, the benefits to the lower back are far more important. The gluteals begin well above the

lowest part of the spine. If they're kept well toned, the whole lower back is more likely to be properly stabilized.

Kneading the buttocks also feels very good. Your partner will usually remind you of that after the first few strokes.

Use the whole flat surface of your hands. For once, you can pick up a generous fold of flesh with your thumbs on each kneading rotation. Squeeze gently. The buttocks can be kneaded separately or combined with a general stroke that includes the whole side of the back (as shown). Start kneading just below the lower ribs and work your way down to the buttocks. On the outside of the thigh, where the gluteals end, reverse the stroke and return to the starting position.

Hip Friction

Once the side and buttocks have been well kneaded, it's easy to reach the deep-set joint at the top of the leg with a penetrating friction movement. Anchor above the joint, opening your thumb wide (as shown). Push inward and down with the top half of the fingers. When you can feel the joint, begin to rotate your hand slowly, spreading friction with the top half of your fingers. Hip friction becomes awkward on the near side of the body. It's best to move to the other side and reach across to massage the opposite hip.

Remember: whenever you change sides, do so quietly while maintaining contact with a single hand or even a fingertip. Throughout every massage, continuous physical contact is crucial. Breaking it interrupts the hypnotic mood you've been working to create, and your partner goes from feeling pampered to feeling abandoned.

Hip friction can also work nicely around the small of the back, where the nerves that supply the legs emerge. Use less pressure here, more speed.

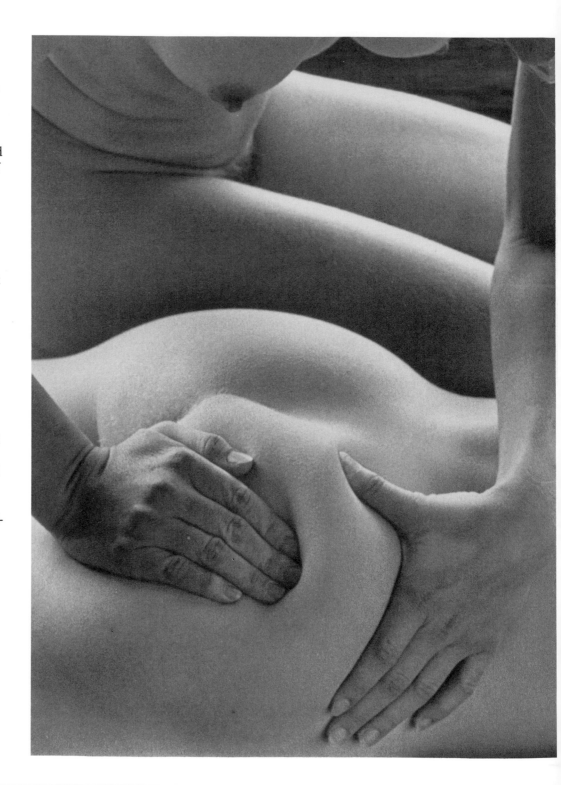

Compression

High Intensity Compression

Compression is even easier to do on the lower back than it was on the bonier neck and shoulders. And it feels just as good.

During this stroke keep the whole side of your leg in contact with your partner's body. A comfortable starting position allows plenty of room to reach the far side of the back and makes it easy to maintain contact if you need to reposition your hands. Oil the whole lower back area, put one open hand over the other, and begin circling. Turn your hands in small circles, use moderate pressures, and cover the whole area from the thigh to the bottom of the rib cage. On this part of the body, compression strokes are enhanced by maintaining full contact from the fingertips to the base of the palm. As your hands turn, push down so that pressures to your contact hand are distributed evenly. (Don't "dig in" with your fingertips.) The heavily muscled parts of the lower back and the buttocks, where the most debilitating cramps originate, will accept deep pressures. Ease up a bit just below the lower ribs, where you're directly over internal organs.

Once you get started, it's easy to continue with compression for a long time. At times, this simple movement feels just as good to your partner as the more complex kneading and percussion strokes.

If the lower back is so tense that ordinary compression movements seem to glide ineffectually over the surface (or if you're much smaller than your partner), use this stroke to intensify the penetrating effect. Heavily muscled types always seem to appreciate the extra pressure.

Make a fist with one hand and press the flat part of your knuckle against your partner's back. Grasp the contact hand around the wrist, then begin turning while pressing down with both hands (as shown). Lean into the movement when massaging thicker muscles, but avoid "digging in" with the tips of your knuckles or the bottom of the palm. Like other strokes that require extra effort, high intensity compression is more effective if you reach across the back to massage the opposite side of your partner's body. Circle slowly.

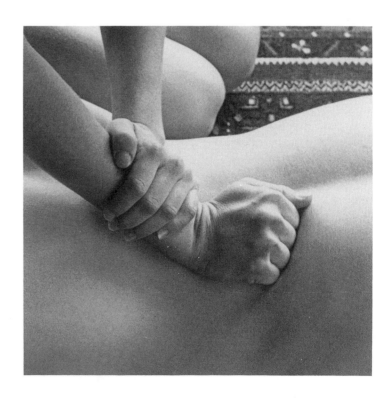

A Half Body Lift

This is one of the rare massage strokes in which physical strength matters. If your partner is much bigger than you, skip the half body lift and instead try one of the back flexes described in Chapter 10. The lift is, however, much easier to do than it looks.

To practice it, prop up your partner's head and shoulders on a pillow — that way if you let go suddenly, the trip down will be a pleasant one. Practice until you can move from the initial lifting position behind the neck to the full upright position without hesitation. As always, pay close attention to how your partner is actually feeling. Try to emphasize the lifting sensation, not the mechanics.

The lower back lift is an effective passive exercise for the massive sacroiliac joint where the bottom of the spine meets the hips. Pressures generated during stress tend to tighten up the muscles and tendons around this joint. Here's a way to reverse those destructive forces.

During the half body lift it's helpful to have a medium-sized flat pillow for your knees. Get comfortable, then stretch your hands under your partner's armpits, clasping your fingers around the back of the neck. Let your fingers meet at the center of the neck, lacing them together if possible (as shown). As you lift, put your front foot squarely on the ground, forming a kind of stabilizing tripod, and be sure not to push forward on the neck — this is massage, not wrestling. All the real pressure is exerted just below your partner's shoulders. Avoiding sudden, jerky movements, pull up slowly until you feel resistance. As always, the point of tension will vary — never force your partner past it. Hold steady at the point of tension for a silent count of ten, then lower your partner slowly to the massage surface. Take a deep breath and try another half body lift. Moving at the same measured speed, repeat the lift at least three times.

Deep Plucking

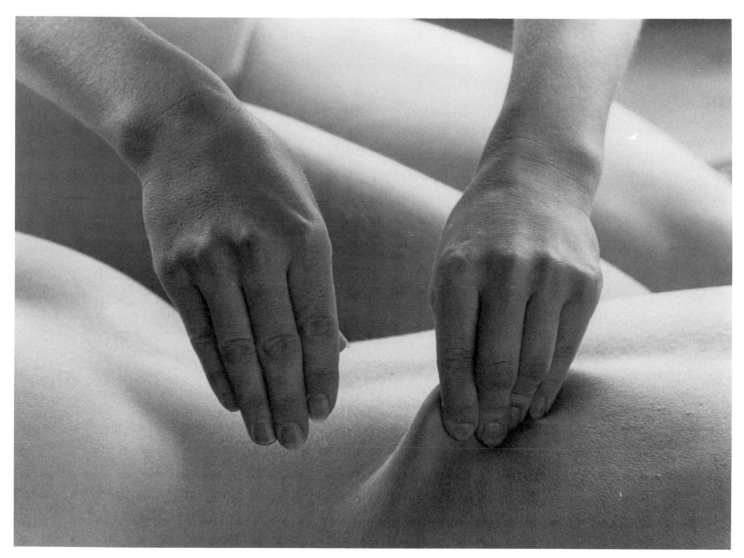

Plucking was supposedly the favorite stroke of Julius Caesar, who used massage to unwind when he wasn't busy conquering the world. From the moment it begins, this unique percussion stroke has a way of commanding one's full attention. Have you been struggling to convince a very self-absorbed individual to find time for massage? Are you trying to find a way around the rush reflex (see p. 98)? Start with a minute or two of deep plucking and your partner should settle down fast.

Push down gently into the soft tissue of the lower back or buttocks to pick up a fold of flesh between your thumb and four fingers (as shown). Lift and then release it. As you release one fold, lift the next with your other hand. By alternating hands like this you can move slowly across an entire fleshy part of the body, plucking as you go. Avoid pinching your partner—the ideal effect is a gentle squeezing. Pluck on the muscular ridges along the spine and below the ribs, but stay off the bony rib cage itself. Plucking works best where the flesh rises easily.

70   Three-Minute Relief from Lower Back Pain

A Full Body Sweep

The luxurious body sweep spreads sensation from the center of your partner's body outward toward the extremities. The stroke begins and ends on the lower back.

Touch your partner's body with your knees — it's easier to reach forward if you sit close to your partner. Press down on the small of the back with the full surface of both forearms. Make a fist with both hands and bend them in against the body (as shown). Every bit of contact during a forearm sweep will magnify the sensation. Maintaining

contact from the elbow to the surface of your fist, move your top arm up to the shoulders while the lower arm descends to the knees. Naturally, the precise finishing point for each arm will depend on the size relationship between you and your partner. Move the arms at the same speed, stopping

only at the furthest extremity and the starting point for a few moments.

Sweep the whole back of the body three times.

6.
Three-Minute
Relief from
Sore Feet

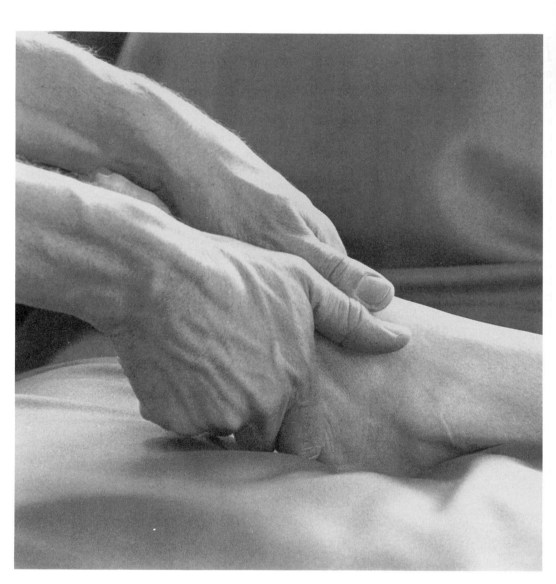

Three essential strokes
One minute each, fifty repetitions

- ☛ Circulation
- ☛ Fast stroking the calf
- ☛ Multiple joint stretching

Complete Peace for the Feet

Most adults haven't been touched on the foot by another person since childhood. Feet, we are led to believe, require little care and are quite incapable of experiencing pleasurable sensations — they either hurt or feel nothing at all. You bind and gag the feet in tight leather shoes, then you step on things; you kick things. Fitness plans usually emphasize the upper part of the body: the face, biceps, waistline, perhaps the hips and legs, while the feet are taken for granted. It's assumed they will perform on demand — nothing complicated is supposed to happen below the ankles.

We usually think of stress as a complex mental state that originates at the very top of the body. In fact, since the feet are richly supplied with nerves from the lower spine, pain that originates, say, in the arch, will travel quickly. Sore feet will sour a good mood in minutes and make pills that knock out the whole central nervous system tempting. If you want to control stress, the importance of relaxing the feet cannot be overemphasized.

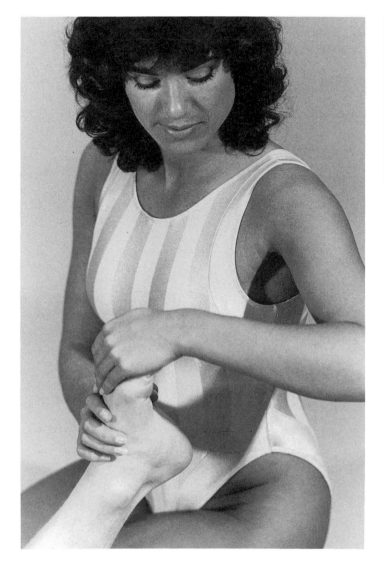

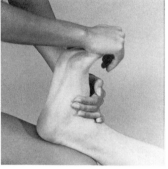

A foot massage is an excellent introduction to the powers of massage. Highly stressed types who would not normally sit still for a massage will always let you fool around with their feet for a few minutes (if only to get rid of pain and restore the feet to their "normal" deadened state). Once you've relaxed and reinvigorated the feet, you'll have a convert who's anxious to test Super Massage on other parts of the body.

A decent foot massage requires some real effort — expect to work up a sweat before you're through.

Circulation

Massaging the top of the foot where the venous system becomes clearly visible, you can see another important element of the fluid release effect at work. Stroking toward the heart accelerates circulation while the heart slows down. This of course is the very opposite of what happens during stress. If your partner is suffering from the effects of vasoconstriction (pale skin, shallow breathing, snappish behavior), try beginning your massage on the feet, the furthest spot in the body from the heart.

Kneel just below your partner's feet, resting the foot you plan to massage against your knee. Wrap your hands around the top of the foot, with the fingers facing in opposite directions (as shown). Keeping your fingers and thumb pressed together, press forward with both hands at once. End the stroke above the ankle or, if you can reach comfortably, halfway up the calf. Maintain contact with the sides of your partner's foot as you return to the starting position. Foot circulation feels especially good at high speeds. Start slowly to establish the form of the stroke (every foot is different), then, smoothly, build

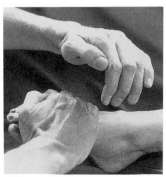

up speed. At faster speeds it feels good to press forward with one hand at a time. Take care not to slap at the foot — whatever the speed, keep your rhythm consistent.

Rotating the Top of the Foot

The feet bend in several places besides the obvious one at the ankles. Notice the clear separation of movement when you rotate a foot at the ankle: the leg remains perfectly still while the foot turns. Near the toes, structures become less flexible, but the joints are mobile enough to stretch nearby muscles, tendons, and ligaments. Here again, you can do things on the bottom of the foot that your partner simply cannot do for himself. During this stroke the top half of the foot will rotate while the bottom half remains still.

To get started, rest your partner's foot on or just above your knee and fold one hand over the top of the toes. Anchor the stroke with your other hand just below the ankle (as shown). Try to isolate most of the movement above the anchor hand.

Determining the point of tension by gently rocking the top of the foot from side to side provides a sense of how much movement is possible. The greatest range of movement is either straight up or straight down, but the whole top of the foot will rotate in an irregular arc. Make at least three complete revolutions in each direction.

Then, using just your thumb and forefinger, grasp the sides of each toe and rotate slowly. Don't rush the toes. It's probably been a long time since your partner has been touched here by another human being.

Fast Stroking the Calf

Since the muscles and tendons that operate the foot descend from the calf, a decent foot massage should start just below the knee. Beginning on the midcalf, the powerful Achilles tendon wraps around the heel, extending all the way to the bottom of the foot. It is the body's largest and most unpredictable tendon. Any tendon can tear unexpectedly, but when the Achilles gives way, proper walking becomes impossible. High-heeled shoes tend to shorten it, while competitive sports stretch it to the limit. Sports masseurs are careful to keep the tendon supple, even if that means spending an extra five minutes a day on the back of the leg. But it doesn't take a rigorous workout to tighten up a tendon—stress can have much the same effect. When exercising, stressed individuals often make the dangerous mistake of skipping a warm-up. If something breaks, it's likely to be the Achilles tendon.

A variety of friction and fingertip kneading strokes work well on this tendon. But if you have time for only one movement, a fast hand-over-hand pulling stroke will warm the whole area and leave it feeling invigorated.

With your partner lying on his back, support the leg just above the knee with a small pillow or simply lift it straight up (as shown). Either way, it's easy to pull back from the bottom of the knee to the ankle, using the whole surface of your hands. Start slowly and build up speed. One hand should be up near the back of the knee while the other pulls down to the ankle. What your partner feels is a single, uninterrupted wave of sensation cascading down the leg. Keep it up for a full minute.

Finish the movement by pulling both hands down the foot all the way to the toes. Then do the same thing on the other leg.

Thumb Kneading the Bottom of the Foot

The bottom of the foot will accept more pressure than almost any other part of the body. One can bear down against the arch with the heel of one hand or, better yet, the thumbs can be brought to bear directly. This is a finger-tip kneading variation, a stroke that is usually reserved for the more delicate parts of the body. Here on the bottom of the feet, however, the powerful muscles of the arch fairly cry out for plenty of pressure. Give it to them with your thumbs.

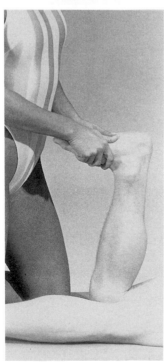

Raise the bottom half of your partner's leg by bending it at the knee. Kneel at the toes or behind the heel when massaging the bottom of the foot. Wrap your hands around the top of the foot, keeping your thumbs parallel on the bottom of the foot. Keep a firm grip on the foot throughout this movement. Pressing down hard, rotate your thumbs on the tough bottom of the foot. Each thumb rotates in an independent circle, just as each hand worked in an independent circle during the full hand kneading strokes (see p. 34). And, again, the circles are in opposition — one thumb is up while the other is down. Moving slowly, cover the whole bottom of the foot from heel to toes. Then return to the starting position. Repeat the stroke three times, then do the other foot.

Deep Compression

Lubricating the Ankle

Your partner may be delighted to discover that the usual pressures on the bottom of the foot can be reversed. If thumb kneading was appreciated, you can amplify the same sensation with this stroke. Lean into a deep compression movement and bear down on the arch with your whole arm.

All that pressure requires a bit of extra control. Avoid bending the foot too far back by kneeling close enough to support it with the front of your knee or a small pillow while anchoring just above the ankle (as shown). Put pressure on the bottom of the foot with the whole flat part of your knuckle and, space permitting, the fleshy base of the palm. Press down hard with your closed fist and begin rotating. Start on the arch, moving up onto the ball of the foot and down to the thick surface of the heel. Stay on the bottom of the foot with this movement. Avoid "digging in" with the sharp part of your knuckles. Turn your hand in small circles, always making as much contact as possible.

No joint anywhere on the body is subjected to greater stress than the ankle. When you exercise, particularly when you run, the ankle is literally pounded from above by the whole weight of the body; nevertheless it must lift and turn without complaint. Stiffness here can lead to all kinds of nasty injuries, the least of which is the well-known sprained ankle. Happily, though, it's easy to isolate the foot from the destructive effects of stress that originates elsewhere in the body. Have your partner lie down on her back, then support the leg with a small pillow under the knee. That takes care of the leg, now you can take care of her ankle.

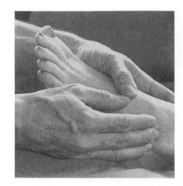

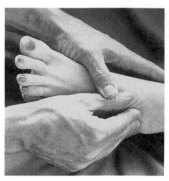

Reach down to your partner's ankle with all four fingers of both hands. By pressing in with the tips of your fingers while circling the ankle, you can combine three very important stress-reduction techniques. First, accumulated acids and other waste products are pressed out of the tissues. Secondly, the production of synovial fluid, an important joint lubricant, is stimulated. And finally, the stroke feels very good.

Circle the ankle four times in each direction. You can sometimes feel fluid draining from the joint as you massage. When that happens, follow the draining movement with a hard four-finger spot friction stroke to the whole calf.

Rotating the Foot

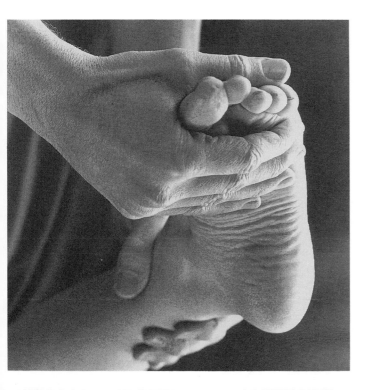

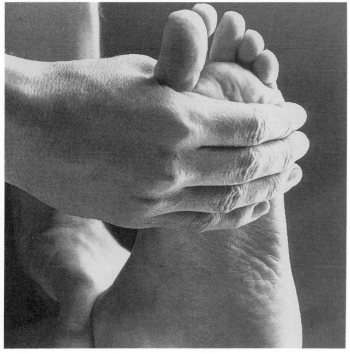

For every ankle that's sprained during a strenuous sporting event probably two are twisted stepping off a curb the wrong way. As stress levels mount throughout the body, tension is transmitted directly to tendons and ligaments inside the joints. The less mobility inside a joint, the more likely painful sprains become. We don't usually think of our ankles after a hard day at work . . . until it's too late.

Sprains can't be entirely prevented with massage, but we can make them less likely simply by keeping the ligaments inside the ankle supple. If a sprain does occur, frequent massage will shorten the recovery time by as much as 60 percent. More on that later. Stretching the ligaments inside the ankle must be done gently. The following foot rotation movement — practiced by sports masseurs all over the world — is an ideal passive exercise for the whole ankle. You do all the work, your partner does nothing at all.

With your partner lying on her stomach, place a pillow under the knee. Lift and support the leg with one hand just above the ankle. Now grasp the top of the foot with your free hand and begin turning it. If you turn from just below the toes, the complex joint at the middle of the foot will be flexed as well. Like all joints, the foot turns in an irregular arc. Test the limits of the arc the first time around, then turn just inside the point of tension. Bend the top of the foot outward (as shown) and rotate it three times in each direction.

Multiple Joint Stretching

With a single movement, the foot can become a useful handle for stretching all the joints from the ankles to the hips. With your partner on his back, hold the top of his foot just below the toes while grasping the heel with your other hand. Lift the foot slightly and, smoothly, pull straight back with both hands at once. As the joints at the ankle, knee, and hip are flexed, the effects of this simple pulling motion can be felt halfway across the body. Pull until you feel real resistance, then hold for a silent count of ten. Release the foot gradually, but just before you break contact start pulling again. That way what your partner feels is an uninterrupted wave of pulling and release, pulling and release. Repeat the movement at least three times on each one of your partner's feet.

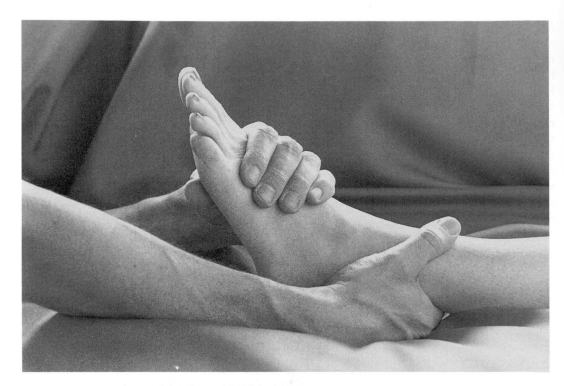

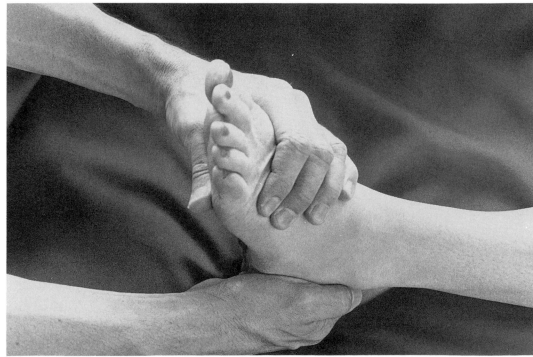

Quick Relief from Sprains

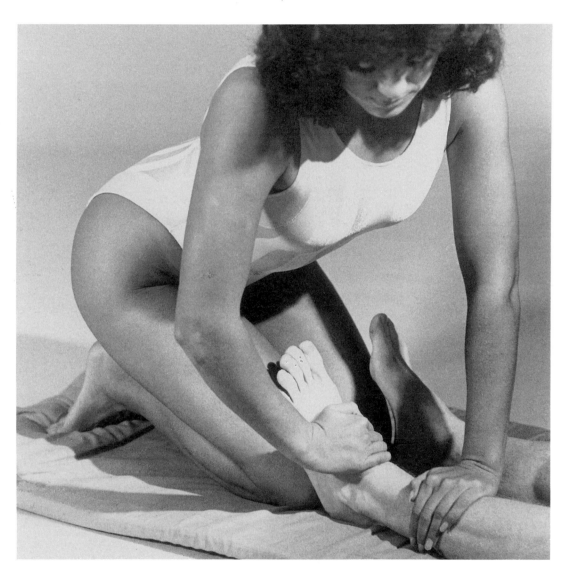

Much of the discomfort of simple sprains comes from the intense concentration of fluids in the injured area. The familiar sprained ankle that swells to several times its normal size cannot recover until the fluids are dispersed. If the pain is considerable, check first with a doctor to be sure a local fracture isn't the real problem. Once you get a medical clearance you can begin massage as soon as the usual cold compress has been removed. You would expect the amazing fluid release techniques that drain wastes from exhausted muscles to be particularly effective around a sprain, and you won't be disappointed. A hundred years ago, when physicians still routinely massaged their patients, Douglas Graham, an American physician, had remarkable success with friction, kneading, and circulation sequences in speeding a patient's recovery from sprains.

Graham records patients with severe sprain under his care recovering the full use of the sprained joint in five days when massage was begun at once. In seven hundred cases of sprains and joint contusions treated by French, German, and Scandinavian army surgeons, comparative statistics reveal that we can reasonably expect that sprains treated by massage will recover in one third the time than those will where the part is kept immobile. — Kathryn L. Jensen, *Fundamentals of Massage*

You'll find nothing mysterious in the techniques that worked so well for Dr. Graham; just a few minutes of hard work are required several times a day. To disperse the irritating fluids, Graham depended on concentrated fingertip kneading from midcalf to midfoot followed by light friction to the joint and a few full hand circulation strokes from the foot to the knee. Use light pressures while the area remains tender and repeat the massage three times a day. As the swelling begins to recede, increase the pressure and frequency of massage. Each session need only last a few minutes. Massaging a sprain will save your partner days of recovery time.

3

LOOK BETTER,
FEEL BETTER,
SLEEP BETTER

7.
Four-Minute Insurance from Wrinkles and Worry Lines

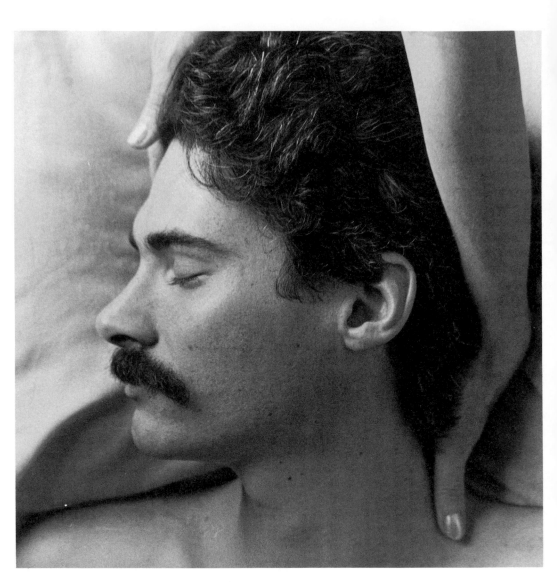

Three essential strokes
One minute each, fifty repetitions

☞ Pressing the forehead
☞ Rotating on the temples
☞ Fingertip kneading the face

Inside the Face

We have seen how stressed muscles are stretched tight, then pumped up with adrenaline and bathed in acids until relaxation becomes nearly impossible. With no relief from tension, the muscles will finally lose their natural resiliency and begin to sag. Small ones usually collapse first, which is why the ravages of stress are so apparent on the surface of the face. But if the source of stress is removed soon enough, fatigued muscles may be able to recover and you will witness a dramatic change; wrinkles that looked permanent begin to fade—transforming the whole face. Every massage facial must deal with a curious, often ignored phenomenon: wrinkles are rarely caused by imperfections in the skin, but rather by a weakening of the underlying muscles. Masseurs who do facials regularly begin to understand several cost-effective facts of life:

1. Mud, clay, and various specialized masks generate a unique feeling. They do not, however, provide a more effective way to clean the face than ordinary soap and water. Too much mud can destroy your hair.

2. Dabbing expensive cream, jelly, powder, oil, sauce, or extract on the face does nothing for existing wrinkles.

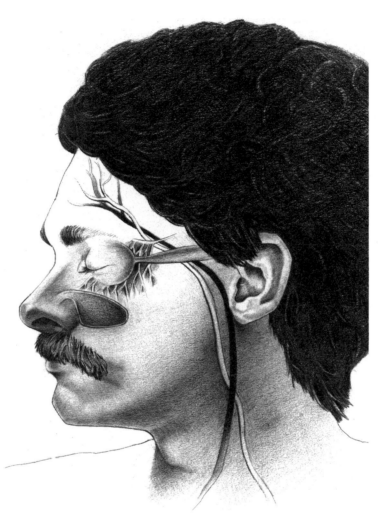

Major nerves and blood vessels converge at the temples.

Too much dabbing can deplete your checking account.

3. Steaming the skin makes it look red for a while. This is not a sign of health, just a sign that the skin has been overheated. Too much steam can burn your face.

4. Contorting the face with specialized exercises once a month or so has no useful effect.

5. Silicone travels.

As certain as death and taxes, when the tiny subcutaneous muscles of expression lose their tone, the surface of the face will wrinkle. Exactly the same thing happens, on a larger scale, around the waist-line or thighs when local muscles get flabby (try rubbing bee jelly on your thighs to tighten them up). Any treatment that is confined to the surface of the body will have little effect on wrinkles. You must reach inside the body to the source of the trouble. With certain modifications, massage techniques for firming up the fleshier parts of the body will work on the face. At its best, a facial massage can actually fulfill the promise of beauty creams and lotions by changing, in minutes, your partner's appearance. Wrinkles and crow's-feet may be permanent or they may be held in place by stress-tensed muscles. You'll find out which one after a first facial massage. Relax stressed muscles and the wrinkles may vanish.

The strokes that follow are focused on the part of the face that controls the precise way your partner looks—the tiny muscles of expression. All the movements are confined to a small area—in some cases just a single finger is used. Nevertheless, the effects can be just as dramatic as strokes that require half an arm. Your partner will feel the difference immediately after you finish a facial massage.

Then he'll see the difference.

A Simple Tension Test

Occasionally, a masseur can discover precisely how much tension a partner has by simply observing the body during massage. Long after local muscles yield to massage, certain parts of the body stubbornly refuse to relax, indicating that stress still rules. One of the most obvious, here on the head, is the jaw. If the mouth refuses to open when you press down gently on the chin, your partner is not relaxed. Resist the temptation to share this piece of intelligence; people do not become relaxed when told to do so. Instead, continue massaging the muscles of the face, adding extra repetitions everywhere you feel the slightest tension. Try pressing down on the chin again in a minute or two. When the mouth opens easily you've succeeded in relaxing the head and face.

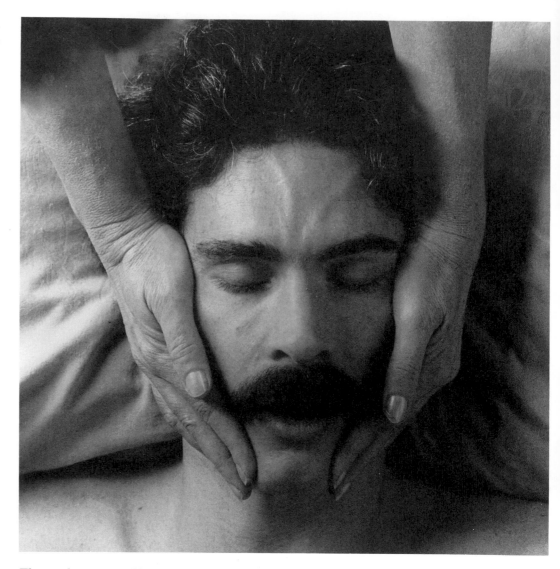

They need to worry and betray time with urgencies false and otherwise, purely anxious and whiny, their souls really won't be at peace unless they can latch on to an established and proven worry and having once found it they assume facial expressions to fit and go with it, which is, you see, unhappiness, and all the time it all flies by them and they know it and that too worries them no end.
— Neal Cassady, *Scenes Along the Road*

Muscle and Mood

When we read a face we're simply noting the current state of the subcutaneous muscles. The tiny muscles of the face, some of the most delicate structures anywhere in the body, are just inches from the brain itself. Normally the facial muscles reflect every emotional nuance, but under stress they will involuntarily freeze into a kind of rigid mask, an effect known as "body armor"; few Americans reach middle age without experiencing it. The supremely animated faces of children can trade tears for joy in seconds, but with the onset of body armor later in life all that changes. Suddenly the facial muscles must go through a ponderous shifting of gears with each new emotion — even smiling becomes complicated. As various moods flicker by during the day, muscles that once stretched effortlessly quiver with nervous indecision. Attempts to moderate the expression inevitably backfire. What good is a stiff upper lip if the lower one is quivering violently?

Tension is contagious. The fact is, if you're carrying too much body armor people start avoiding you. An expression or two can be faked, but,

as every actor knows, the transitions *between* expressions are much more difficult. Facial body armor doesn't respond to creams, ointments, lotions, or powders. The only escape is to relax the tiny subcutaneous muscles of the face; five minutes of work for your masseur.

Say you're so nervous before a very important meeting that you feel like climbing the walls. You find yourself pacing back and forth in your office like a caged animal. All that tension goes directly to the muscles of the face, where it becomes terribly public the moment the meeting begins. If you can't relax, others will find it difficult to do so as well. Suddenly, instead of sharing ideas you're sharing anxieties, and the whole tone of the meeting is changed. The next time you get wound up before a meeting, lean back and close your eyes for five minutes while somebody massages your face. Unwind with Super Massage. You'll go into the meeting rested and relaxed; your face will be more natural, more convincing.

Scalp Friction

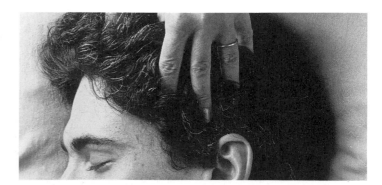

Think of the scalp as the top of the face. If your partner is tense the scalp will feel tight, and that tension is transmitted directly to the delicate muscles of the face. You can't hope to relax the face if the scalp is tense.

Be sure your partner removes earrings and contact lenses before you begin massage of the scalp and face. When you're planning on massaging with oil, do this stroke at the beginning while your hands are still dry. Reach into your partner's hair and press down against the scalp with your fingertips — careful not to pull the hair. Other friction movements avoided bony parts of the body; this one seeks them out. You should be able to feel the surface of the skull throughout scalp friction. Don't rub the scalp, push through it against the bone. Test the movement a few times before you begin. Scalp friction works best if you press the thumb and four fingers toward each other repeatedly. Move slowly from

the front of the hairline all the way to the back of the skull. After a few passes you will feel a tangible difference in the range of available movement beneath your fingertips.

Once the scalp becomes more supple, press down against it with the flat part of your open hands and circle, first with one hand then the other. Half the scalp will move under each hand.

Scalp massage also benefits the hair. Just beneath the surface of the scalp a rich group of blood vessels supplies the roots of the hair. After a few minutes of vigorous scalp friction the scalp is so oxygenated that the hair takes on the glossy textured look one usually expects to see only after an exercise session.

Pressing the Forehead

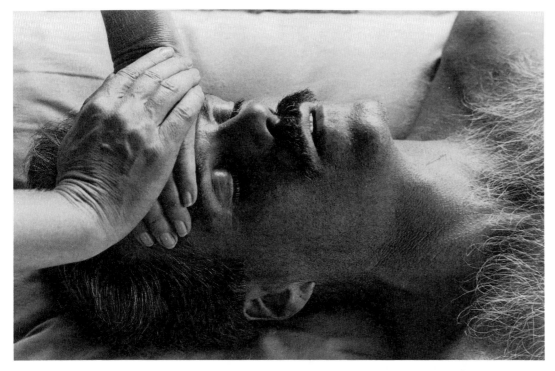

Have frontal headaches been a problem for your partner? This sumptuous two-hand press puts direct pressure on the whole surface of the forehead from temple to temple. Directly under your hands a large set of nerves emerges from the brain. Steady pressure will effectively soothe them.

Support your partner's head from below with a soft pillow, then get comfortable yourself. Sit above the top of your partner's head, close enough so you can reach all the way down to the chin. Carefully establish contact with one hand from temple to temple, distributing pressure from the fingertips to the base of the palm. This is your contact hand, the other hand is called the pressure hand. Adjust your contact hand until the pressures from the fingertips to the base of the palm are equalized. When your hand feels comfortable and well fitted to your partner's forehead, bring down the pressure hand on top of it. Press moderately hard from above with your pressure hand. Hold at the point of maximum pressure for a silent, slow count of ten or twenty, then release your hands very slowly. Repeat this sequence three times — that's often all it takes to get rid of some frontal headaches.

But whether or not the pain disappears right away, continue with facial massage for a while. Everyone wants a relaxed face.

Rotating on the Temples

If you do nothing else on your partner's face you should at least rotate your fingertips on his temples. Stressed people automatically reach for the temples to get relief, but it feels so much better if somebody else does it for you.

Begin by pressing down lightly on the middle of the forehead with your thumbs. Then bring your fingertips around to rest on the two temples. Locate the definable ring of bone surrounding the temples and massage just inside the ring. Depending on the size relationship between your fingers and your partner's head, two, maybe three, fingertips will fit comfortably inside the ring. Reach for the soft inner tissue. You can rotate both hands in the same direction or move in alternating directions — one hand circles up while the other moves down. Maintaining contact with your thumbs at the center of the forehead ties the stroke together and adds to your contact area. Facial strokes on the jaw, sinuses, eyes, and cheeks all begin with the thumbs centered on this spot. As various strokes move out from the center of the forehead, your facial massage acquires symmetry.

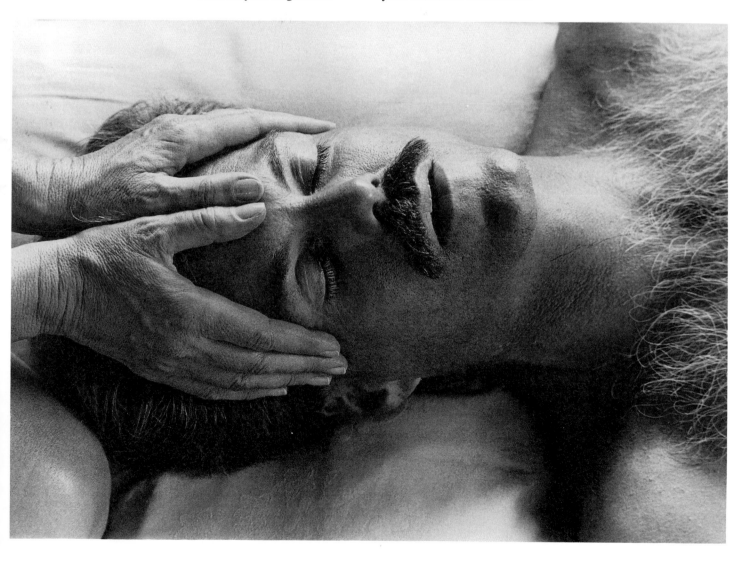

Fingertip Kneading the Face

Stroking the Sinuses

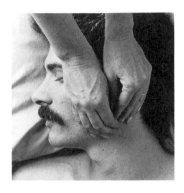

Kneading the muscles of expression is one of the most delicate operations in massage. Your partner will be very aware of *your* mood, so take an extra moment to compose yourself before starting—a gentle, confident manner is always helpful. Oil carefully; one or two drops on the fingertips will do. Have a soft towel ready to take off any excess.

Since the whole skull can move at almost any time during a facial massage, it's especially important to anchor each stroke. People are simply not accustomed to being touched anywhere on the head. However, the face, one of the most sensitive parts of the body, grows accustomed to massage rapidly. This stroke spreads sensation from the temples down to the jaw.

Knead the face from the corner of one eye to the chin. Pick up a tiny fold of flesh between your thumb and forefinger. Near the forehead you will be limited to two fingers, lower on the cheeks you can add one or two more. Avoid pinching or forcing the skin up. The rhythmic kneading motion here is exactly the same as it is on the fleshier parts of the body.

The thumbs and fingers of one hand pick up a fold of flesh while the fingers of the other hand remain open. Cover a whole side of the face from the forehead to the chin, kneading in small circles. This area is small enough to permit easy repetition of any stroke that your partner enjoys. At the back of the jaw, just below the ear, you will always feel a certain amount of extra tension. In fact, the muscles of the jaw are one of the points where stress registers first. Knead it a few extra times. You'll be returning to the jaw muscles soon with more specialized movements. As you knead your partner's face, subcutaneous circulation is stimulated and the muscles beneath the skin grow more supple. Kneading prepares the face for the strokes to follow.

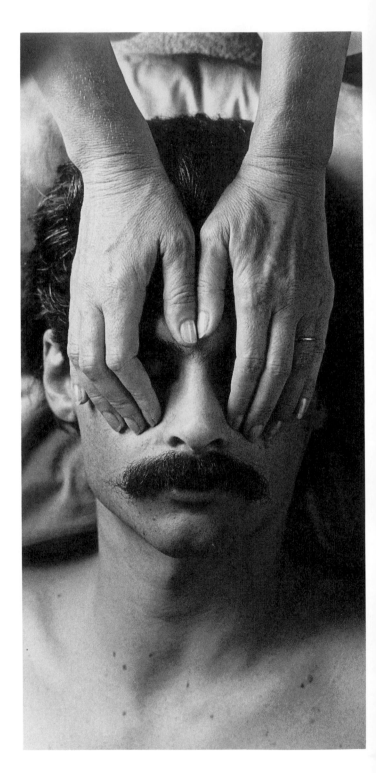

Friction to the Jaw

One of the more unfortunate side effects of stress is a nagging low-level congestion — cold symptoms without the cold. The general tightening that closes down the vascular system during vasoconstriction also affects the sinuses. Breathing becomes more difficult, the voice breaks, and the throat is cleared to no avail. The best solution is to relax the whole body, but one can sometimes achieve satisfying results by massaging the area around the sinuses. Relax the face, and your partner's congestion may vanish.

Begin, once again, by lining up your thumbs at the middle of the forehead. The eyes, like the temples, are set inside a ring of bone. Below the bottom of the ring, almost against the nose itself, you can feel the tissue soften. This is just below the spot where the lower sinuses begin. Reach down into that soft spot with your middle finger and trace an arc outward under the bony ring (as shown on p. 90). Then trace the same arc with all four fingers. Repeat the arc with all four fingers, staying just below the bone, at least three times. After the third repetition, reach into the sinus area with two fingers of each hand and apply spot friction. Finish with a long, leisurely forehead press.

The muscles of the jaw are one of the first areas of the face to register stress. Once the most powerful muscles of the face become tense, a kind of negative undertow is exerted on surrounding tissues. You see the effects immediately around the corners of the mouth and eyes, where smaller muscles are literally pulled out of shape by the inflexible jaw muscles. And they will stay that way, forming all kinds of alarming wrinkles, until the jaw is relaxed.

Center your thumbs on the middle of the forehead and reach down to the base of the jaw with all four fingers of each hand (as shown). The contact area for this spot friction movement is just below the ear and slightly forward. Have your partner grit his teeth for a moment and you will feel a marked muscle concentration at the base of the jaw; this is the precise spot to focus your friction stroke. Anchor the head on one side of the face while applying pressure with your friction hand on the other. Rotate all four fingertips against the thick jaw muscles and don't be afraid to use extra pressure. After massaging one side of the jaw, turn the head slightly, and massage the other side of the jaw. You may want to cover each side of the jaw several times before moving on to the next stroke.

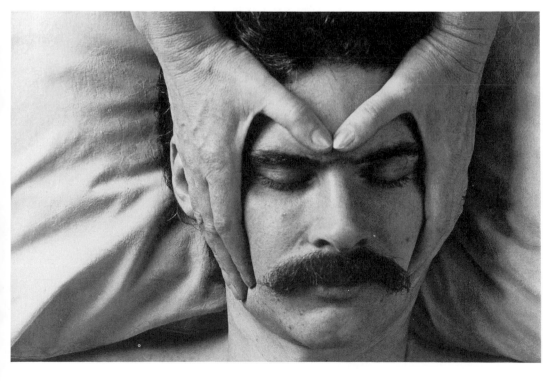

Relaxing the Muscles of Expression

Tension is stored in the shoulders, scalp, and jaws, but it registers first around the eyes and mouth. The muscles here are simply too delicate to resist the powerful forces exerted from above and below during stress. When they yield, people start looking stressed all the time: the expression freezes, smiling becomes awkward, and where clear-eyed serenity once prevailed, a half dozen cross-purpose facial twitches suddenly appear. Happily, if you start massaging soon enough, all of these nasty afflictions are only temporary. Once you've relaxed the neck, scalp, and jaw muscles, you're ready for the tiny, exquisitely sensitive muscles of expression.

Again, most strokes will work best if you keep the thumbs centered on the middle of the forehead. Reach down with your fingers to do the massage.

The muscles of the face before and after massage.

The Eyes

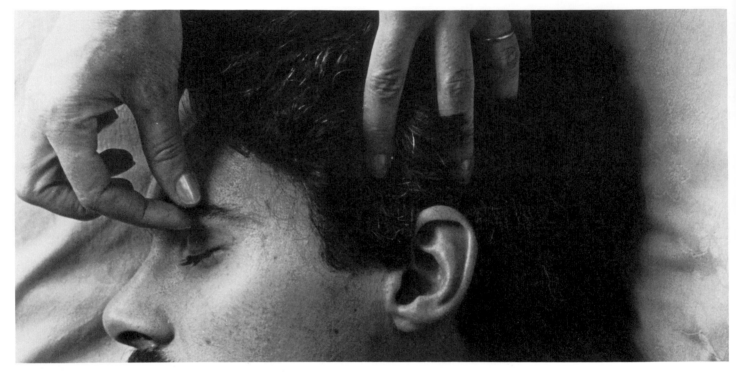

Eye massage works above and beside the eyes as well as directly over the eyelid itself (the thinnest-skinned part of the body). Begin directly above the eyebrow with a four-finger friction stroke. To isolate the effects, anchor close by over the other eye. Rotate your friction hand in tiny circles. The skin will form tiny folds in front of your hand. Move back and forth across half the forehead, then switch hands so you can apply friction above the other eye. Then reach down and do the sides of the eyes with what is, really, a variation of the temple stroke. To get closer to the eye your rotating hand works outside the bony circle.

This is the home of the infamous crow's-feet wrinkles. As you massage, depleted muscles are flooded with oxygen while acidic wastes are driven out of the tissues. Sometimes you can actually see your partner's coloration change from a pale, sickly hue to a vibrant glow as you massage.

Did you know that you can actually put down all four fingers on the top of your partner's eye? Direct eye massage is a delicious experience, all the more so since most people have never even con-sidered it. Center your thumbs on the forehead, then carefully lower both little fingers onto the inside corners of the eyes. Move out toward the corner of the eye, resting the balls of your fingers against the bony upper rim of the eye. Very light contact with the eye is sufficient. As the little finger begins to move, bring down the other fingers one at a time. Turning the hands as your fingers slide out toward the corners of the eyes permits all four fingers to descend and glide, one after the other, across the eye. As you repeat this stroke, return to the starting position and try it on the bottom rim of the eyes.

The Cheeks

The Mouth

This movement will distort your partner's lips into some strange and wonderful shapes. Relaxing the general area around the mouth makes strokes for specific muscle groups at the corners of the lips far more effective.

Begin by extending one hand against a cheek, holding it still, and rotating with the other hand on the opposite cheek (as shown). Once you get a sense of how far the cheeks will move, begin rotating both hands. With your thumbs centered on the forehead, reach down to the cheeks and rotate slowly, using the flat surface of all four fingers. The stroke works best when the hands turn in opposing circles: one hand up while the other is down.

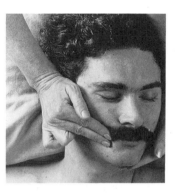

Normally one of the most animated and mobile parts of the body, the area around the mouth is always noticed socially. When the expression changes it usually happens here first. In stressful situations, however, local muscles are kept so unnaturally taut that their resiliency begins to disappear. When relaxation finally does come, the face simply collapses. Precisely because it is so visible, this is one of the most distressing stress patterns anywhere on the body. Stress begins to pull the expression out of shape at the corners of the mouth. Here's how to put it right.

Once again, don't massage the mouth until you've relaxed the larger muscles of the face and shoulders. Tension here is always amplified by outside forces.

Anchoring on the side of the face gives extra support to your partner's head throughout this delicate movement. Reach down to the corner of the mouth with the forefinger and middle fingers of one hand. Right next to the corner of the lips you can feel the spot where the muscles converge. Press there and begin rotating your fingertips, first in one direction then in the opposite direction. This will momentarily distort your partner's features, but, in fact, the rubbery effect is exactly what it takes to restore the natural mobility of the face. Turn your partner's head to one side and, beginning at the corner of the lips and working outward, knead each side of the mouth with your fingertips (as shown). Then turn the head to the center and grasp both cheeks with the whole surface of your hands. Rotate slowly. Finish with a hand-over-hand pulling stroke, starting at each corner of the mouth and ending all the way back at the base of the ear. Maintain tension on the corner of the mouth as you pull.

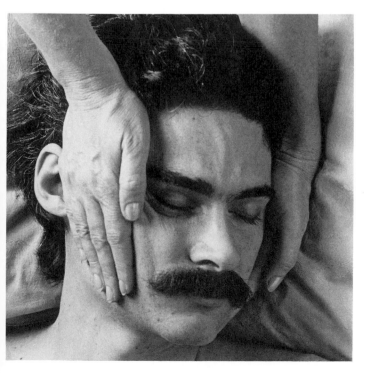

8.
Four-Minute Relief from Nervous Tension

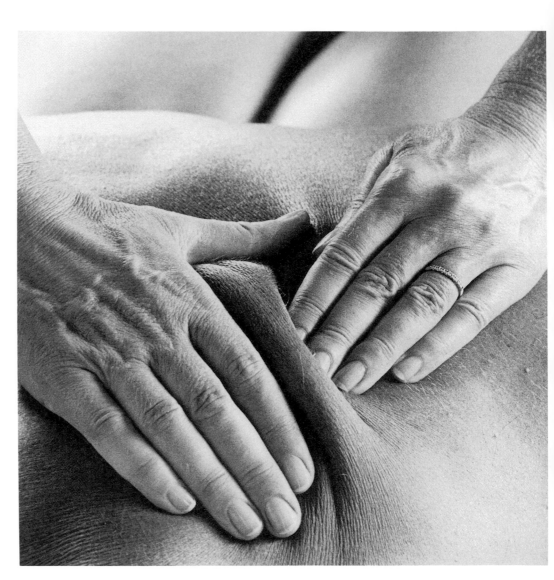

Three essential strokes
One minute each, fifty repetitions

- ☛ Local (or full body) circulation
- ☛ Spot friction
- ☛ Pounding

Massaging the Stress Addict

He seemed to look at us from a zone of weariness where not even despair is felt, because that is feeling, and such weariness is fathoms deeper than feeling.
—C.J. Koch, *The Year of Living Dangerously*

Probably the most difficult challenge you will face when massaging overstressed people will come from the individual who must constantly rush in order to achieve meaning in life. He needs a massage badly but never manages to find time for one. It's so much faster to gulp a few aspirin or tranquilizers, then rush off to the next appointment. The very fact that he's always rushed is supposed to show how committed, successful, and thoroughly modern he is. Snappish, combative, obsessed with clocks, he wears his perpetual tension like a badge of honor. He's the latest medical time bomb, the stress addict.

In the office, on the farm, or in the kitchen, the stress addict is eternally far behind schedule and rushing like mad to catch up. Whenever you meet him you feel pressured: you're wasting his time, you're doing unimportant things that could have been finished long ago, *you're never busy enough.* Alcoholics and drug addicts can sometimes manage to leave the

Do

Ask your partner to close his eyes.
Give your partner permission to relax and do nothing for five minutes.
Keep preliminary conversation to a minimum.

Don't

Give orders. Instead, make suggestions.
Argue about anything.
Talk about how good it will feel after the massage.
Discuss massage techniques.

rest of us alone for a while — not the stress addict. He enjoys bugging other people; he actually seems to thrive on conflict and arguments. Nevertheless, family and friends are often deceived or intimidated by a busier-than-thou air which accompanies almost all activities.

At first, the stress addict may simply appear to be a committed, rather ambitious individual to whom time is money. He's dynamic, perhaps a bit too intense, driven, and fiercely competitive. He finds tension motivating, adrenaline exciting, and delays of any kind infuriating.

Those who live with him, however, soon discover other, more disconcerting traits. He bolts meals, races through meetings, hurries conversation without listening, and charges into lovemaking as though it were an Olympic competition. Vacations and leisure-time activities become a marathon of high-pressure events with winners and losers at every turn. Music, art, and literature hold little interest — they're too time consuming. In fact, nothing matters as much as the process of rushing itself. If something can't be rushed it isn't worth doing.

The rush reflex:

- ☛ Heart rate increases.
- ☛ Blood pressure increases.
- ☛ Adrenaline increases.
- ☛ Arteries and veins contract.
- ☛ Bodily secretions decrease.
- ☛ Oxygen supply to the brain decreases.
- ☛ Judgment and thought become erratic.

- ☛ Muscle tone decreases.
- ☛ Subcutaneous facial muscles collapse, causing early wrinkles.
- ☛ Digestion becomes slow and incomplete.
- ☛ Body experiences constant fatigue and anxiety.

Inside the stress addict an invisible stopwatch ticks away, reducing each day to a series of deadlines which, like hurdles in a hundred-yard dash, must be executed at precisely the right moment. Family, friends, and co-workers with other ideas are accused of being dull, slow, or lazy, then pushed relentlessly. Spare time is for new activities so that additional deadlines and schedules can be crammed into every uncommitted moment. All opportunities for leisure are instantly eliminated. Work hard, play hard.

The stress addict wears his tension like a medal from an honorable war. He's fought the good fight and earned the right to a perpetually stiff neck and six cross-purpose facial twitches. You'd be tense, too, if you weren't so lazy. Finally, when rushing becomes a kind of reflex almost as automatic as breathing, the inevitable physical penalty must be paid: whole sections of the body become permanently tense and everything starts to hurt. Unwinding is then so physically difficult it is all but abandoned.

What remains is a furious scrambling from one deadline to the next, attempting to achieve the stress addict's ulti-

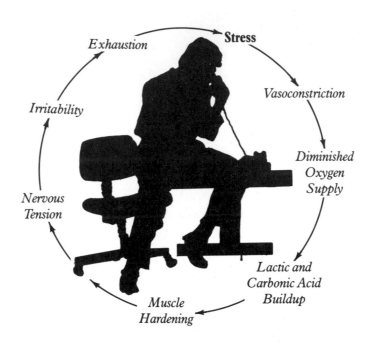

Exhaustion → **Stress**

Irritability *Vasoconstriction*

Nervous Tension *Diminished Oxygen Supply*

Muscle Hardening *Lactic and Carbonic Acid Buildup*

mate goal: *total busyness.* Exhaustion, which sets in late at night and sometimes yields to sleep, takes the place of relaxation. During the day stress generates more stress as all problems are solved by pressuring somebody. "The squeaky wheel gets the oil," insists the stress addict as he bellows out an order, checks his watch and, grabbing at the phone, swallows a handful of Valiums.

The confirmed stress addict invariably blames others for his problems. He needs faster cars, faster food, faster service, and faster-acting pills. He also desperately needs relief from lower back pain,

nagging headaches, persistent neck and shoulder tension, and sore feet. He's having frequent digestion problems and his blood pressure is rising. How do you get him to sit still for a massage?

Not by talking about it. Trying to talk the stress addict into slowing down is frustrating because he will lie (like other addicts) when confronted with his excesses. Things are always "crazy" at the office but the job is "great." Marathon weekends in the country, which might

include eleven hours of driving plus a daunting roster of sports, specially prepared meals, entertainment, and leftover office work are "fun, relaxing." Again, like other addicts, he tries hard to feel superior to everyone else. His life is so "full" compared to yours.

The first clear sign to all that a stress addict has been pushing the limits can, of course, be a heart attack. Of all the debilitating effects during stress none is more dangerous than the abrupt venous and arterial contraction known as vasoconstriction. When adrenaline is squirted into the blood vessels, the entire venous system immediately contracts. The heart then speeds up in order to force blood through the body, and all secretions decrease. The pulse grows weaker and the skin turns deathly pale as blood moves away from the surface. This is the "fight" impulse that permits mammals to become ferocious at a moment's notice. It isn't meant to continue for days, weeks, or months at a time, and when it does the body must pay. Stress addicts learn to enjoy the adrenaline rush and try to ignore the pounding heart that goes with it. The aches and pains, the frequent infections, the insomnia, and the shattered relationships are harder to ignore.

Three Steps to Prepare the Stress Addict for Massage

Masseurs look for a solution to stress addiction inside the body. The immediate problem—muscle tension so pronounced it may be near spasm—is physical, not psychological. Eventually, as co-workers, family, and friends fall behind, the stress addict is driven entirely by his own adrenaline; the body becomes a stress factory. Masseurs seek to change all that by dealing with what the stress addict is actually feeling.

What does it feel like to walk around in his body all day long? The terrific tension in the neck, shoulders, or lower back broadcasts the answer. By focusing on the stressed area with Super Massage, you can reverse the vasoconstriction effect in just a few minutes. Relaxation then takes the place of tension—you substitute one set of feelings for another.

A stress addict can get so wound up that he forgets the difference between tension and relaxation; resting becomes rushing less. Discussing this, however, will only provoke an argument and postpone the massage. Again, *never comment on how tense your partner seems to be.* A better approach is to begin with a simple three-part sensory-awareness exercise that feels so good it becomes a part of the massage.

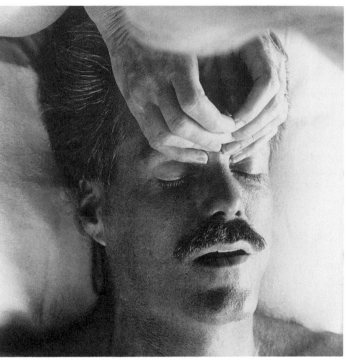

Silence

Since doing nothing may be the greatest sin for a stress addict, it sometimes helps to provide assurances that it's OK to relax. When you do, be prepared for a strange reaction. Ordinary relaxation can be so threatening that to find familiar territory your partner may try desperately to start a stress-generating argument—whatever it takes to get the adrenaline going again. Most masseurs have seen a stress addict, about to surrender and melt as a massage begins, suddenly become completely rigid, sit bolt upright, and demand the time of day. Moments later he's on his feet, searching frantically for his watch, appointment book, and a phone. Giving a stress addict permission to relax is a crucial point in your preparation. By proceeding diplomatically you can defuse an argument, calm irrational fears, and greatly enhance the massage. Here's how.

Most likely the last time your stress-addicted partner experienced real play, leisure, or idleness was as a child. If he's got problems as an adult, why not let him be a child again? Begin by giving your partner permission to relax while playing a simple children's game called "Stiff as a Board." He begins by walking like a wooden soldier, exaggerating each movement. Then, on command, he sits on a rug and immediately becomes a "limp noodle," so limp that he cannot support any part of his body and must collapse to the floor. Repeated several times, this little fantasy clearly demonstrates the difference between tensed and relaxed muscles. Next time you "give him permission" to relax, just before the Super Massage begins, he will know something about how it should feel. And he won't fight the feeling when it starts to happen. The final time your partner becomes limp, ask him to do so without speaking. Silence quiets the mind and allows the feeling of relaxation to take over.

Darkness

Accomplished as the stress addict may be in other areas, his sensual awareness is crude. He will focus on the loud, the aggressive, and the speedy. Simply closing the eyes, as though he were in the presence of an exotic scent or exquisite music, will tune your partner into a more subtle level of sensual awareness. It also releases him from a host of familiar demands. Turn off the lights. Darkness intensifies the sensual.

Breathing

Slow, rhythmic breathing is a luxury that stress addicts almost never allow themselves. It's far too relaxing. By simply asking your partner to breathe deeply during massage you allow her to "do something" while relaxing.

You make breathing into a little job. Still, it's important that your partner realize that breathing itself is not goal oriented. You won't be asking her to increase the speed or giving her other special instructions. It's not a test she can somehow fail. Later, when you do the massage, you can adjust the rhythm of your stroking to your partner's breathing. Right now it's enough just to breathe deeply and slowly.

Quietly, in the warm darkness, your partner will surrender slowly to the natural rhythm of her own breath.

Are high-strung individuals condemned to be forever jittery? It's tempting to dismiss constant nervousness as a stubborn personality trait that simply cannot be changed. It's not. We have seen how a few minutes of Super Massage can transform acid-ridden, fatigued muscles and dramatically improve your partner's mood. At no time are the positive mood swings more apparent than when massaging nervous people.

Masseurs view nervous tension as a physical, not a psychological problem, and work through the body to bring relief. The muscles,

nerves, and brain are so intimately connected that any irritation to one system instantly affects the other two. After many hours of tension, oxygen levels in the muscles are seriously depleted, which means that paralyzing cramps can strike at any time. One can cope with jittery nerves but not with the excruciating pain of cramped muscles. Think of nervous tension as a valuable warning sign: relax the body when muscles begin to tighten, and you should be able to spare your partner the painful cramping that will otherwise inevitably follow.

Strokes in this chapter should be chosen according to your partner's profession and sex. Active and sedentary people experience different kinds of nervous tension. More on that later. When massaging tense women, pay close attention to the pressures you use—a woman's nerves are usually more easily stimulated than a man's. The strokes that follow are designed to provide quick ways of altering tension-induced anxiety and depression. Think of nervous tension as the fuse, and cramps, stomach disorders, and circulatory problems as the bomb. Taking a few minutes to cut the fuse of nervous tension can alter your partner's whole day.

Spot Friction

While most massage movements can travel from one part of the body to another, spot friction is designed to focus on a single tense location. It's useful on the heavily muscled parts of the back as well as in areas where working with the whole hand is awkward. Hard-to-reach nerves just beneath the shoulder blades and at the base of the skull are common sources of headaches and other nervous complaints. Focus on them with spot friction whenever you're dealing with nervous tension.

To be truly effective, friction strokes require plenty of repetition. Get comfortable before starting so you won't have to interrupt the stroke. Generally, women experience tension in the neck and shoulders while male complaints center on the lower back. Check with your partner to find out if any painful areas require special attention.

Uncontrolled spot friction can shake your partner's

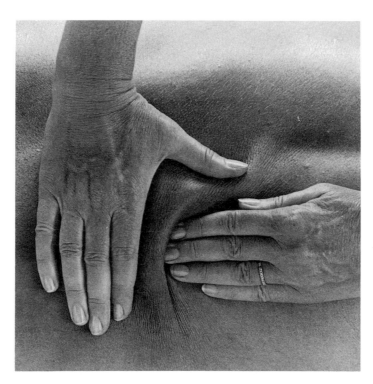

whole body. Confine movement to a single location by pressing a small fold of flesh toward the friction area with one hand (the anchor hand) while you apply friction with the other. Open your thumb whenever possible (as shown). Forget about oil. Remember that friction strokes turn against interior tissues instead of gliding across the surface of the body like other massage movements. Keeping your thumb tight against your

forefinger, press down with your fingertips until you feel muscles beneath the skin. Then, with your fingers pressed tightly together, rotate against the muscular surface. Circle, choosing a moderate speed that you feel comfortable maintaining for a minute or more.

Full Body Circulation

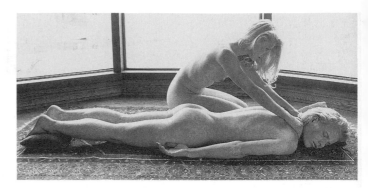

This is the most ambitious stroke in massage. It's also, often, the most appreciated. Get it right and you can treat your partner to one of those delicious experiences that is unique to massage: an uninterrupted wave of sensation traveling all the way from the bottom of the feet to the neck, turning across the shoulders, then returning along the sides of the back and legs to the feet. He *was* experiencing nervous tension. All at once he's experiencing pure pleasure.

Unless you're much bigger than your partner you will need to change position several times during a full body circulation movement. Spread out a few small pillows along your partner's side and move as quietly as possible. Remember: the best masseur, like the best waiter, is invisible. Bend your fingers, throughout this stroke, to follow the changing contours of your partner's body.

Begin on the bottom of the feet. Cup your hands around your partner's foot with your fingertips facing each other. Press up onto the calves and across the back of the knees to the upper thighs (as shown). Then, without interrupting the stroke, move forward, repositioning yourself near your partner's waist. As you move up the back, your fingertips should come close to touching the sides of the spine. At the base of the neck, let your fingertips turn until they are pointing toward

the ground. Move out to the edge of the shoulders, turn again, and begin your descent along the sides of the back. Careful not to cut corners at the feet — your partner will notice if you rush. Continue down all the way to the toes, then turn your hands and get back into the starting position with your fingers facing each other.

Take your time and let your partner savor the ascending and descending waves of sensation. Repeat the whole movement three times. After your final return to the feet, if your partner asks for more, it's easy enough to keep going.

Vibration — a Spot Friction Variation

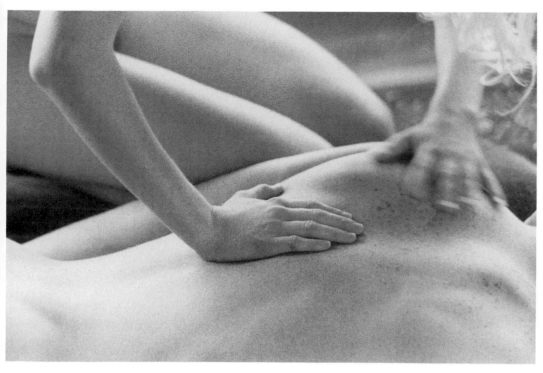

Nervous tension usually spreads from an irritable area to the whole body. Before you begin massage, see if your partner can pinpoint certain spots that feel more tense than others. Work on them first. If it's difficult to isolate tension in a single area, start by paying special attention to the neck and shoulders, the small of the back, and the muscular part of the calves.

You can choose one of two spot friction variations. For deeply knotted interior muscles you will need to press down fairly hard as you turn with a regular spot friction movement. But if the skin seems taut and the muscles beneath are slack, tension is probably limited to the surface of the body. Try a minute or two of vibration, an open-fingered friction variation that produces a pleasant glow across the surface of your partner's body.

Vibration breaks one of the hard-and-fast rules of massage: it's done with the fingers spread apart. However, you do make use of nearly the whole surface of each finger throughout the stroke. Anchor near the friction area with one hand. Since you won't be pressing down into the tissues, don't bother picking up a large fold of flesh with the anchor hand. Simply concentrate on confining the effects of the vibration to a single area. Holding steady with the anchor hand, turn your vibration hand rapidly from side to side at the wrist. Be sure to break the movement at the wrist. Vibration with the whole arm becomes awkward . Let your fingers brush across the surface of your partner's body as you turn the vibration hand. As you approach the side of a limb, bend around the curve with your fingers.

Move as fast as you can while maintaining a comfortable rhythm. As always, consistent rhythm is more important than raw speed. This stroke allows you to blanket a joint or muscle group with intense sensation for a minute or more. When you stop, your partner will realize that cold, clammy tightness has yielded to a warm, spreading glow.

Full Hand Cupping

Pounding

Eventually, nervous tension will dominate almost any personality. If your neck and shoulders are seldom relaxed, you're simply not going to feel very good about life. Massage brings relief via the fluid release effect and by substituting an intensely pleasurable experience for the enervating tension. Tense people are impatient, even snappish, so you need to reach inside the body and make things happen fast. One way to do this is with a series of high-intensity percussion strokes.

Full hand cupping works on most broad, fleshy areas, but it's especially effective on the heavily muscled parts of the back. Cup your hand (as shown) to form a small hollow area in the center. When contacting your partner's back, listen for a slight popping sound as a tiny vacuum is formed between your hands and the surface of the body.

As in all percussion movements you must cushion each "blow" by breaking the downward thrust at the wrist. Move up and down the sides of the back, methodically keeping your hands close enough for the thumbs to brush each other. Cover the whole back up to the muscular ridges that run parallel to the spine, but stay off the spine itself.

Pop, pop, pop. Full hand cupping brings blood to the surface where you can see it.

Pounding really comes into its own on the back. Massaging from the center of your partner's body (as shown), you can usually reach from the midthigh to the shoulders. Pressures should vary depending on what's under your contact hand. Reserve your lightest strokes for the soft area between the lower ribs and the hips.

Pounding is a versatile stroke: you can cover an entire leg or limit the effects to a single aching muscle group. Either way, the effects reach deep within the body to interior muscles, nerves, even organs,

The Pinky Snap

providing the dramatic changes you need to eliminate nervous tension.

Obviously one can get carried away with pounding. Cushion the stroke two ways: first, by striking the back of your contact hand instead of your partner's body, then, by breaking the downward thrust at the wrist. Pounding is most effective if you reach across the spine to massage the far side of your partner's body. Use your contact hand to feel for bony areas like the rib cage and shoulder tops before you begin. Never pound on the spine itself. To focus on the long muscles that run parallel to the spine, it's important to limit the pounding to your fingertips. Let the palm of your contact hand ride lightly over the spine while pressing down on the muscles with your fingertips. Then pound the back of the fingertips with your other hand.

Thanks to Hollywood, the pinky snap (a.k.a. hacking) is probably the most misunderstood massage movement. We see it in movies while people talk on the phone, drive, eat, and play cards — in short, always while doing something else. Suddenly the neck and shoulders are besieged with a flurry of quick karatelike chops to the soft tissue while the vital pinky snap, which is supposed to moderate the blow, is invariably left out. No wonder the obligatory sigh of pleasure afterward seems false — a little closer to the spine and the scene would become impossible to reshoot.

Real pinky snapping is always cushioned by the little finger, which hangs down as the hand descends. Actually, there are two cushioning points during this stroke: at the pinky and at the wrist. When bringing each hand down, make sure to break at the wrist. The effect you want is a light, snapping motion. One hand is always up while the other is down.

An agreeable rhythm is more important than raw speed, so find a comfortable rate of repetition and stay with it. As the pinky closes against the fingers, listen for a crisp snapping sound — when it's consistent so is your rhythm. The stroke should move slowly across the body, covering each area thoroughly. Dazzling jumps from, say, the upper back to a leg à la Hollywood may impress onlookers, but will confuse your partner. On the other hand, repeating the stroke over a small area three or four times provides a pleasant warming effect that will last for hours.

Pressing the Spine

Muscles along the nerve-rich spine are extremely sensitive to stress. In fact, when tension persists, the lower back is one of the first parts of the body to suffer. Women generally experience tension around the neck and shoulders; for men the most sensitive area is the lower back. Normally, the vertebrae are held in place by the long muscles that run parallel to the spine. When stressed, however, the muscles tighten, pulling, even jerking the spine to one side. A vicious circle of mounting tension then begins: direct pressure to the spine irritates the nerves, thereby causing more muscle contraction which, in turn, generates more stress. Eventually, an excruciating lower back muscle spasm can result. If the pain is intense always check with a doctor before beginning massage.

Once you're satisfied that there's no structural damage, use back pressing with fingertip kneading and friction movements to relax over-tensed muscles and bring peace to the lower back. Sometimes you can actually feel the muscles soften as you massage.

There are several ways to press along the spine. Both hands can rise together to the shoulders, spreading sensation evenly, or the hands can ascend one at a time, limiting the sensation to a single side of the back. Either way, confine your pressures to the raised muscular ridge that runs parallel to both sides of the spine. Stay off the spine itself. Push forward into the muscle with the heel of your hand. Lean into this stroke. Flatten out your hands at the shoulders and move out across the shoulder tops. Maintain light contact with your partner's sides on the return to the waist.

Vibrating the Whole Upper Body

It's always best to be sure the neck is relaxed before doing this stroke. If your partner struggles to "help" when you start lifting the head, her neck is still very tense. Remind her, gently, not to help when she feels her head being lifted. You do all the work — she does nothing at all. If tension remains, spend a minute or two fingertip kneading the thick muscles at the base of the neck (see p. 47). Lift again and repeat the neck kneading if necessary. When your partner's head falls back gracefully as your hands press up between the shoulders, she is ready to surrender to the luxurious feeling of being lifted into the air while her back vibrates slowly.

Kneel above your partner's head. Oil your hands, then slide them under her shoulders, spreading the oil as you move, down to the area between the shoulder blades. Begin by simply lifting up with the fingertips of both hands until the rib cage begins to rise. The vibration effect is produced by raising and lowering your fingers rapidly. Keep your fingers pressed tightly together and pull up toward the neck as you vibrate. Once you get comfortable with the pulling-up motion, try increasing the frequency so what your partner feels is a subdued percussion from beneath the ribs. Pull your hands up toward the neck as you vibrate. This stroke moves in only one direction: from the shoulders to the neck. Return to the starting position between the shoulder blades each time you reach the neck. Reach halfway down her back for the final lifting-pulling sequence. Feels as great as it looks.

9.
Four-Minute Relief from Insomnia

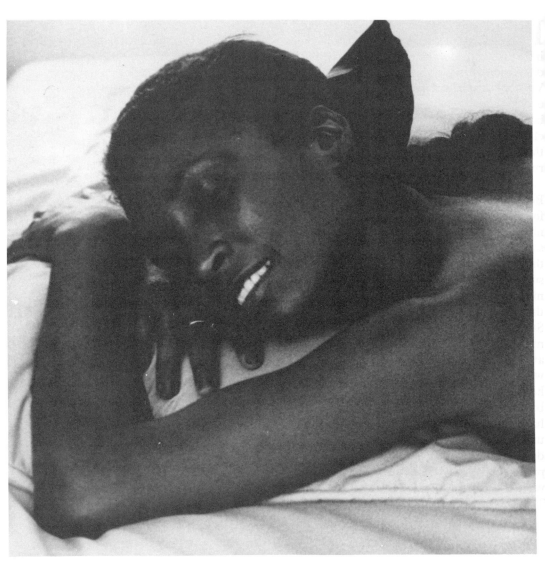

The feeling of loneliness and depression that is so apt to come in the nighttime when people are run down or in ill-health is usually dispelled very promptly by means of massage. In this and other respects its action is similar to the primary and agreeable effects of opium and alcohol in restoring tone to the respiratory centre and vascular system, without, however, the injurious aftereffects of these internal remedies. In place of headache, drowsiness, and disordered digestion, which are so apt to result from the use of hypnotics and stimulants, after sleep from massage the patient is refreshed and buoyant in mind and body. Massage does more than this: it will often counteract the disagreeable feelings that result from the necessity of taking sleep-producing medicines or too free indulgence in alcoholic stimuli. —Douglas Graham, M.D., *A Treatise on Massage*

Massage at Midnight

Perhaps no malady is more closely tied to stress than insomnia. How does one slow down after rushing all day? When the tensions of the day end up in bed, unwinding becomes yet another stressful chore. But, of course, sleep is the one goal that cannot be rushed or forced.

Bedtime is an ideal setting for massage; a comfortable mattress, a darkened room, silence. For centuries only the rich and powerful could summon a masseur at midnight. A hundred years ago the President of the United States, arguably one of the more stressed individuals around, found that sleep would come in minutes when he had himself massaged at bedtime. We now depend on habit-forming drugs with unpredictable side effects to do the same thing. Certain pills will knock you out, but what about the next morning? The massage solution has no unpleasant side effects.

Take a few special precautions when massaging an insomniac. Be careful not to be distracted by nervous conversation. Your focus should remain on the body, especially on the limbs, where poor circulation can leave the muscles very tight. Avoid the natural tendency to favor very delicate movements, which seem more soothing late at

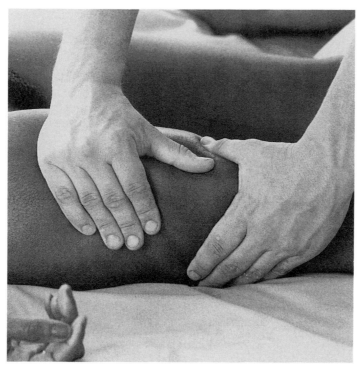

Do

Keep the lights low.

Take the extra time to heat the oil.

Be sure to keep your partner warm; use blankets on part of the body if necessary.

Give extra attention to the limbs.

Be silent.

Be generous with massage.

Don't

Discuss your partner's problems.

Complain about being up late.

Make the experience complicated. Skip the food, drinks, music, magazines, and aspirin. This is massage, not air travel. If all goes well, your partner will be asleep very soon.

Stop massaging the moment breathing becomes regular. Asleep, your partner's body continues to benefit from the massage.

night. Insomniacs are almost always *over*stimulated. The more flamboyant massage movements, even strokes that vibrate over large parts of the body, are more likely to break a mental logjam and relax the muscles. The larger, more dramatic massage movements will also distract your partner from nagging anxieties. Remember: the brain has been racing, generating stress at a furious rate. With massage you create physical events, tangible *feelings* that are far more immediate and significant than any kind of mental static.

If it's been a particularly stressful day for your partner, you may have to disperse large quantities of irritating acidic wastes. Concentrate on repeating the kneading and circulation sequences in this chapter wherever you find tensed muscles.

Professional masseurs take it as a compliment when a client falls asleep during a massage. What better sign could you get that tension has been relieved? (The only problem is finding a graceful way to make room on the massage table for the next client.) If your partner does drift off after a minute or two, continue massaging for a while. It's not the conscious mind you're working on, it's the body.

Energize the Limbs:
Super Circulation

The adrenaline released by stress dilates blood vessels in our muscles so that blood drains from our body to our legs.
— Dr. Claire Weekes, *Peace From Nervous Suffering*

We have seen how stress constricts the circulatory system, trapping irritating acids deep within the muscles. Eventually, when the muscles are not permitted to relax, the acidic buildup itself becomes a source of stress. The body is under constant attack from within. At the end of the day, when stimulants and mood enhancers wear off, tension should finally yield to exhaustion. But what if some of the stress-hardened muscles refuse to relax and sleep doesn't follow?

During most insomnia episodes, stale, poorly oxygenated blood and various toxins clog the limbs, producing a leaden feeling that is especially troublesome in the legs. Before your partner will feel any real relief, you must clear irritating acids from the tissues and reinvigorate both legs. A high-intensity circulation movement will immediately oxygenate the legs, eliminating the "deadness" in less than two minutes.

Begin with a series of rapid circulation strokes. Start at the ankles and press all the way up to the buttocks. At

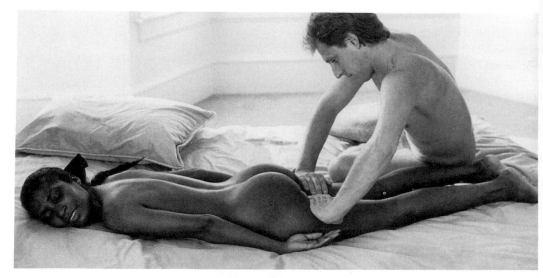

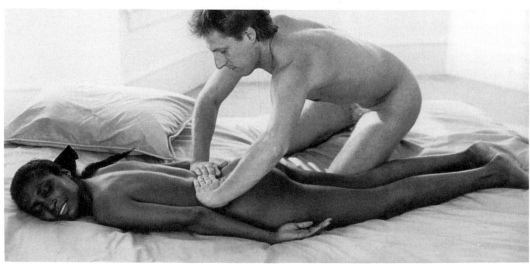

the hips, turn your fingers out and return to the ankles, maintaining light contact on the sides of the legs. Do each leg separately at least twenty times, then finish up with three or four luxurious full body strokes, covering both legs at once. At the top of the last circulation stroke, continue up over the buttocks

(as shown) and across the back all the way to the shoulders. With light, full-hand pressure, turn your fingers out again and return to the ankles down the sides of your partner's body. Maintain full contact with your hands when turning at the feet and shoulders. A full body stroke allows your part-

ner to feel truly pampered. As you move up and down the body, you may need to reposition your body. Do so without breaking the rhythm of this, the longest of all massage strokes. Feel for knotted muscles along the whole length of the body. That way you know exactly where to begin with the next stroke.

Relief for Tensed Muscles: Compression

Rock-hard muscles cry out for a minute or two of compression. Often, you can actually feel them soften under your hands.

This is a friction variation, so you will need to anchor from above or below. You can do compression on the back or the back of the legs without oil, but it usually works better with light lubrication (particularly if your partner has hairy legs). Make a fist and press down firmly with the flat part of your knuckle. For a softer effect, press down with one hand on top of the other (as shown). Turn slowly as you press. Confine yourself to the thigh on the front of the leg—from the knee down it's too bony. Compression really comes into its own on the muscular back of the leg. Here you can begin just above the ankle and work up all the way onto the upper back.

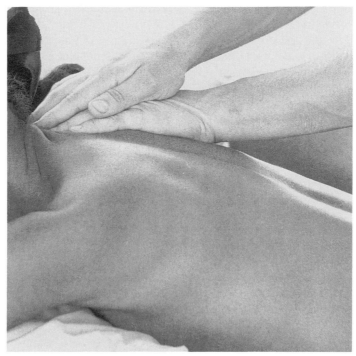

One area bears special watching during back-of-the-leg compression. The Achilles tendon, largest tendon in the body, wraps around the heel and extends halfway up the calf. If it's too tense the whole leg will be affected. Be sure to circle all the way down the heel itself when you're massaging the lower part of the leg. If the tendon feels tight and requires extra attention, put a small pillow under the ankle to raise the foot.

Deep Friction

Ask your partner how she feels. If she's uncertain, do a final full body circulation stroke, checking, once again, for knotted muscles. Again, insomniacs have trouble pinpointing exactly what is bothering them. Feel for the tension. Are the muscles of the neck rigid even when the head is supported? Do you feel more tension on one side of the spine than on the other? Does the calf remain tight when the rest of the leg is relaxed? You've found the spots where she needs deep friction.

Skip the oil. Keep in mind, during friction, that unlike most massage strokes, your hands should *not* glide across the surface of the skin. Friction movements rotate on the muscles beneath the skin. Feel for them; let the muscles, not the skin, ripple under your fingertips as your hand turns. On the thicker leg muscles, press down with the flat part of your knuckles; use just your fingertips over the long muscles that run parallel to the spine. Anchor the stroke with one hand as the other applies friction (as shown). Start slowly and find a comfortable pressure for

plenty of repetition. It's tempting to push down very hard on larger muscle groups, but the extra pressure can tire you out. When poor nighttime circulation depletes the oxygen supply inside major muscles, extended friction is a wonderful gift. Take a break with a light fingertip kneading stroke, maintaining contact and rhythm while

you get ready to do some more deep friction. If there are no specific complaints, concentrate on the lower legs, where circulation is likely to be the poorest. Three or four rotations on tensed muscles make a difference—one hundred and the tension vanishes.

Flexing the Legs

With your partner lying on her stomach, lift both her legs at the ankles, bending her knees until the feet are straight up. Fold the ankles over each other (as shown). Then grasp both ankles and press down slowly until you feel tightness. The point of tension, where you feel a tangible strain, will vary from one individual to another. The heels can touch the buttocks without a trace of resistance or they can grow tight just a few inches beyond the upright position. Once it's established, the point of tension indicates just how far to press the legs without causing discomfort. On the upward part of the stroke, take the legs all the way back to the original position with your partner's feet on the bed.

Then, lift with both hands and press again. After repeating this movement a half dozen times, press *slightly* beyond the point of tension just once. The legs can also be flexed from the other side of the body by simply pressing forward against your partner's knees (as shown).

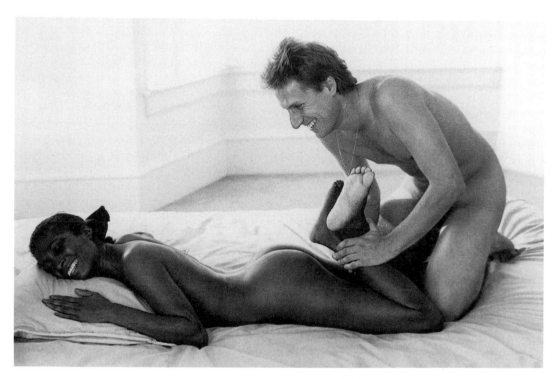

Knead the Whole Side of the Body

Once you've relaxed the legs and applied deep friction to areas of obvious tension on other parts of the body, your partner will probably be more than halfway asleep. Try some more of the luxurious full body strokes. Be generous when massaging an insomniac. An extra few dozen repetitions will go a long way toward relaxing her.

Reach across your partner's body and knead the entire opposite side. Start at the ankles and move all the way up to the shoulders. Pay special attention to the fleshy areas around the hips. Whenever possible, use the whole surface of your hands from the fingertips to the base of the palm. Between the rib cage and the knees you'll find it's easy to pick up a fold of flesh between your thumb and forefinger with each stroke. On the bony sides of the knees and near the ankles don't bother forcing the flesh to come up if it doesn't do so easily. But whether or not the flesh is actually lifted, keeping the thumb movement consistent with each stroke maintains the hypnotic mood you're working to create. When kneading the side of the body, you can relax muscles that operate the arms, legs, and back (as shown).

Shaking the Body

Does your partner complain of feeling stiff in bed? No reason to let that keep her awake. Here is a simple lift that flexes the major joints of the lower back and hips while your partner does nothing at all. As the whole center of the body rises slowly, feelings of tension give way to an expansive light sensation.

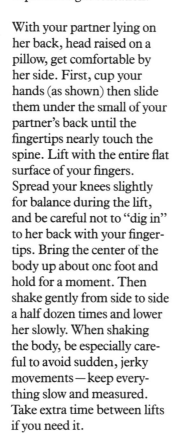

With your partner lying on her back, head raised on a pillow, get comfortable by her side. First, cup your hands (as shown) then slide them under the small of your partner's back until the fingertips nearly touch the spine. Lift with the entire flat surface of your fingers. Spread your knees slightly for balance during the lift, and be careful not to "dig in" to her back with your fingertips. Bring the center of the body up about one foot and hold for a moment. Then shake gently from side to side a half dozen times and lower her slowly. When shaking the body, be especially careful to avoid sudden, jerky movements — keep everything slow and measured. Take extra time between lifts if you need it.

Lift and shake three times. Then, maintaining contact with a knee or one hand, sit back, rest for a moment, and watch your partner smile. Levitation is the perfect escape for insomniacs.

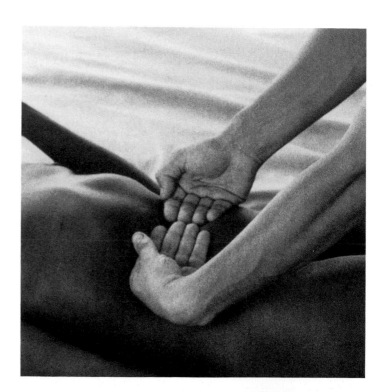

Thumb Kneading

Squeezing and Rolling the Arm

Sometimes insomniacs are able to identify a single source of tension, such as a stiff neck, a sore arm, or aching muscles in the calf, which calls for a single, concentrated massage solution. Thumb kneading, one of the most adaptable strokes in massage, is ideal for all these problems. It's especially

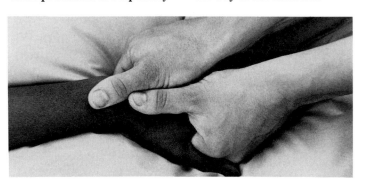

effective in tight areas that full hand kneading strokes can't reach.

Thumb kneading works best on the limbs, although it can be adapted for parts of the torso as well. Reach under the limb with all four fingers of each hand, resting your thumbs on the surface (as shown). Rotate the thumbs in opposing circles: one up while the other is down. While you knead, try to keep the thumbs as close to each other as possible without pinching the flesh.

Thumb kneading travels well. With your partner lying on her stomach, you can begin kneading the Achilles tendon at the ankle, move up the fleshy back of the calf, and end on the broad surface of the thigh. Or start at the wrist, move up the inside of the forearm, and knead all the way to the shoulder.

Always knead the soft, fleshy areas—avoid the bony parts of the body.

A unique thumb kneading variation sometimes called "the violin" frees up both of your hands to massage the upper arm. It also elevates the upper arm while you massage it, which makes the stroke considerably easier to do. Lift the arm you want to knead and put all four fingers under the armpit, the thumb on top (as shown). Holding your arm tight against your body as you knead will keep your partner's hand in place.

If your partner enjoyed body shaking, these two arm movements are sure to please. They stimulate without becoming jarring and they do wonders for aching arm muscles. Here is something unusual for your partner to *feel* instead of something abstract to worry about. See these movements as a simple alternative to anxiety as well as one more step toward eliminating the irritability that comes between your partner and deep sleep.

Circle the wrist with your thumb and forefinger, then lift your partner's arm straight into the air. Reach over with your other hand and circle her arm near the shoulder. Squeeze between your thumb and four fingers. Concentrating on the soft tissue areas, move up the arm all the way to the wrist. Squeeze every second or so.

Rolling also begins near the top of the arm, but with an important difference. This time you use both hands to bring the sensation surging upward. First, fold your partner's arm across her chest (as shown). Then, with your fingers straight out, reach forward and grasp both sides of her upper arm as close to the shoulder as possible. Gently at first, then more vigorously, rock your hands back and forth as they move up the arm. Your partner's arm will straighten at the elbow as you move up toward the wrist. When you reach the wrist, lower her arm, supporting it above and below the elbow with both hands, and begin again from the starting position.

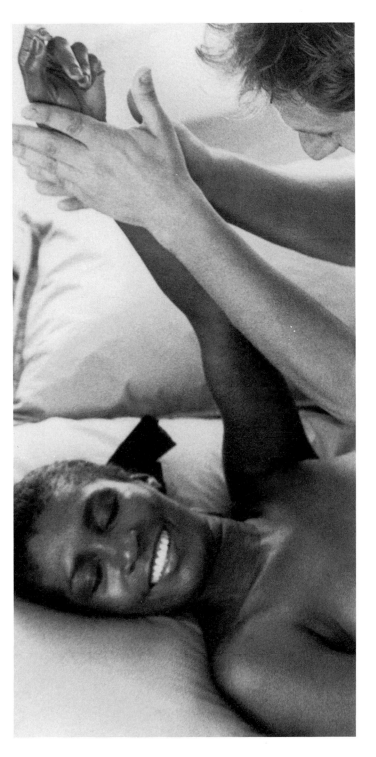 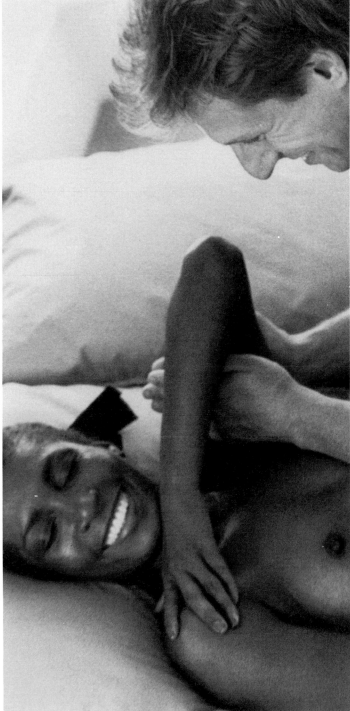

Fast Stroking the Whole Leg

Brushing the Body

Covering an entire leg with a series of quick full hand strokes, this movement is the longest fast stroking variation anywhere on the body. It's an ideal way to complete a leg massage; your partner experiences waves of sensation moving from the top of the leg to the bottom.

Reach straight down and grasp the top of the thigh with both hands (as shown), bringing your thumb around as far as it will go comfortably. Pull down, hand over hand, as far as the knee, then over the knee onto the lower leg. Stop at the ankle. Build up speed gradually once you get comfortable. Pressures should be light to moderate, even at high speeds, during this stroke. The trick is to grasp the leg firmly without grabbing at it. As you move closer to the feet, reposition yourself quietly without interrupting the movement. What your partner should feel (again, the final test of any massage) is a cascading wave of sensation beginning near the hip and descending all the way to the feet.

Fast stroking—the decisive way to move off a leg.

To be lomi-lomied *you lie down upon a mat or undress for the night. [A native], beginning with your head and working down slowly over the whole body, seizes and squeezes with quite peculiar art every tired muscle, working and kneading with indefatigable patience. . . Whereas you were weary and worn out, you find yourself fresh, all soreness and weariness absolutely and entirely gone, and mind and body soothed to a healthful and refreshing sleep.* —Charles Nordhoff, *Northern California, Oregon, and the Sandwich Islands*

Generally, massage during insomnia ranges from deep, penetrating strokes to very light contact. The most delicate stroke of all is the delightful full body brushing movement. Save it for the end.

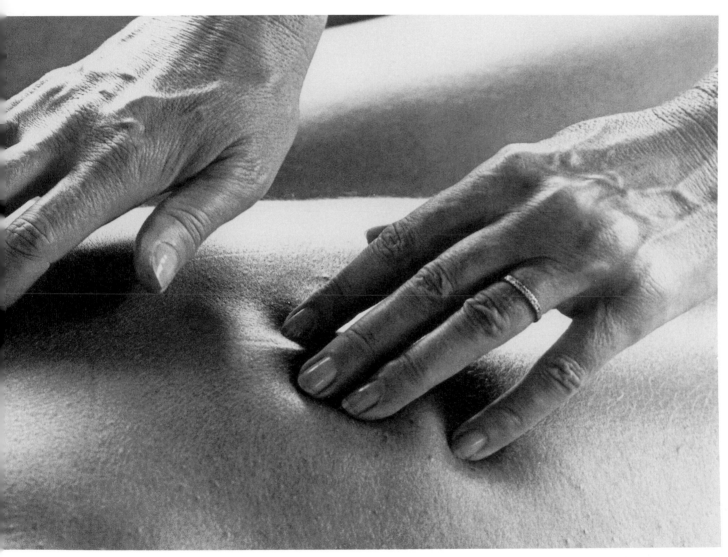

Begin by centering your hands at the top of the spine just below your partner's neck (as shown). Simply hold your hands in place for half a minute or so without moving. Open your fingers and begin moving down the spine with one hand, then the other over the same route. Two hands following each other enhance the sensation. Make contact only with the tips of your fingers. Brush slowly, pulling straight down the spine, covering each area several times as you descend. Continue over the buttocks and move down the backs of the legs. The feet are especially sensitive to a light, brushing movement, perhaps because most people cannot remember the last time they felt anything light or delicate on the feet. Complete the stroke with your fingertips in contact with your partner's toes. Pick one toe for your final contact, the same one on each foot. Now the stroke stops again, just as it did at the beginning of the movement. Maintain single-finger contact with a single toe on each foot for a silent count of ten. Then, very slowly, break contact.

Be silent.

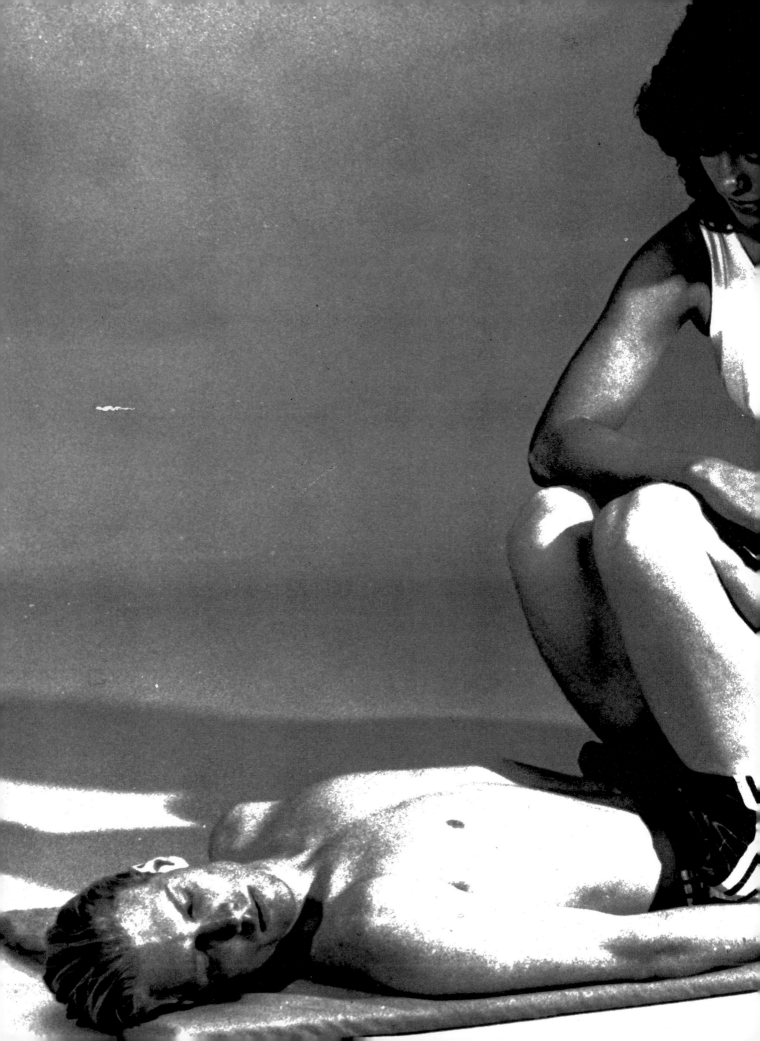

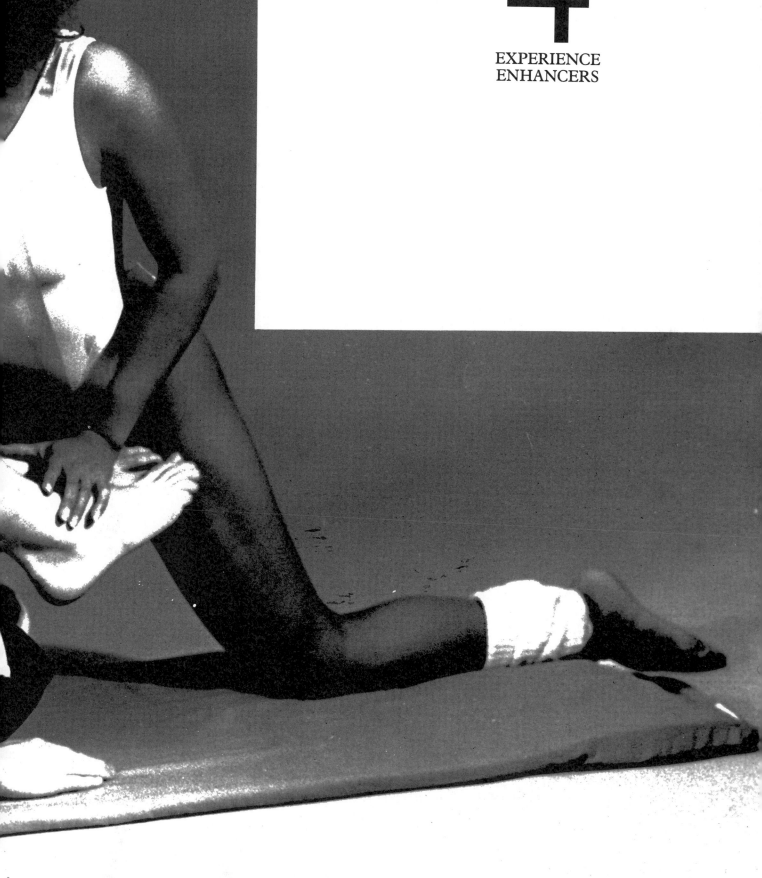

4
EXPERIENCE
ENHANCERS

10.
Five-Minute
After-Exercise
Conditioning

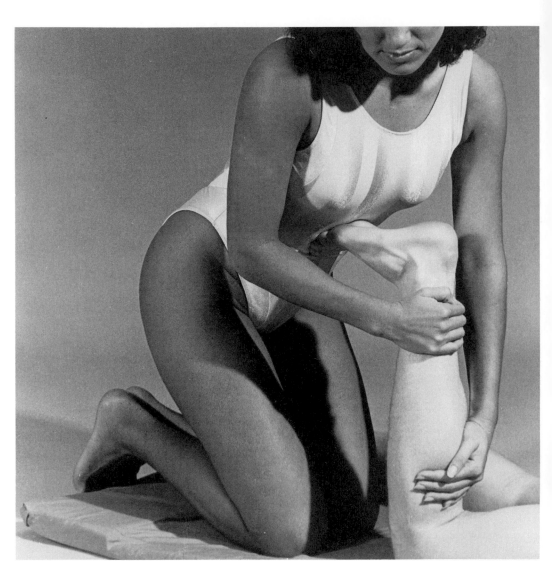

Three essential strokes
Three minutes each, fifty repetitions

☛ Flexing the top of the back
☛ Pumping the legs
☛ Forearm percussion

Exercise Without Pain

Fitness programs, especially those designed for the novice, come with a hidden cost: when the exhilaration that follows exercise begins to fade, nagging aches and pains can pop up all over the body. You get up an hour earlier to run, only to discover that your knees hurt all day. An invigorating bicycle ride leaves your legs so tense that sleep becomes difficult. And we're told that this is exactly as it should be — getting in shape means living with an aching body. In fitness, as in life, there is no gain, according to the joyless Puritan ethic, without pain. Eventually, pain becomes an end in itself, a sought-after goal — press on until your muscles burn, because only then are you finally getting somewhere. Staying fit is reduced to an excruciating ordeal, something one endures like unpleasant medicine "because it's good for you." Suffer or get fat.

We know that the dreaded lactic acid, a by-product of increased combustion rates during exercise, will irritate the muscles for hours, even days, after a workout. The question is: are aching, acid-drenched muscles the price we *must* pay for fitness?

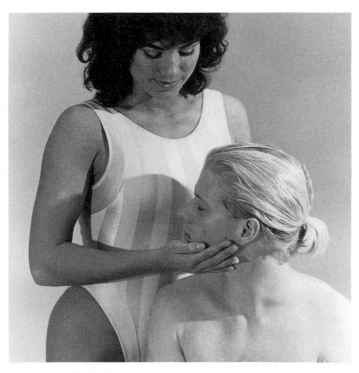

Ergographic tests, used to measure muscle recovery rates after exertion, point the way to the missing link in the modern exercise program; a specialized kind of Super Massage that works in stages. First, the enhanced blood supply created by massage acts as a natural analgesic; it relieves pain. Then, once tensed muscles begin to relax, circulation strokes become far more effective, boosting the oxygen content of tissues in the massaged area by more than 15 percent. Extra oxygen means irritating wastes can be burned off more quickly, but a more significant change comes about when you concentrate on eliminating the cause of after-exercise pain.

During Super Massage, when lactic acid is literally squeezed out of the muscles, the normal metabolic process is accelerated. In minutes, you can accomplish what it would take hours or days for the body to do by itself. After the massage, your partner goes through the day invigorated instead of in pain. But there's more . . . don't stop massaging when stress-hardened muscles begin to yield. By continuing for just a few more minutes you will discover why Olympic teams all over the world have become intensely interested in massage.

The effects of several minutes of Super Massage on fatigued muscles simply has to be experienced to be believed. Again, typical muscle recovery rates after exercise are no more than 20 percent. A person capable of doing fifty push-ups will, after five minutes of rest, be capable of doing only ten more. But if five minutes of fluid release

After-exercise massage:

Relaxes tensed muscles.
Oxygenates internal tissues.
Boosts the combustion rate of acidic wastes.
Increases the white and red blood cell count in the massaged area.
Boosts the muscle recovery rate from 75 percent to 125 percent.

Flexing the Top of the Back

massage is substituted for the five minutes of rest, muscle recovery rates jump to between 75 percent and 100 percent!*

Originally documented by scientists more than eighty years ago, this significant data was largely ignored by generations of antitactile Americans. Until very recently serious athletes were expected to put up with aching muscles after every workout. In 1980, when I introduced a program of fluid release massage for runners in *The New Massage*, only a few teams throughout the world traveled with a masseur. Not surprisingly, the East Germans, Israelis, and (a few) American swim teams who massaged their athletes dominated the competition. The news spread with their track records, and today nearly every major competitor recognizes the value of massage as a natural training aid. All over the world, swimmers, runners, dancers, weight lifters, and boxers have discovered a drug-free way to radically alter the effects of fatigue on the muscles.

One way to overcome the puritanical fear of massage is to start with a dramatic effect that cannot be duplicated in any exercise program. At first, back flexing feels more like exercise than massage, but you will notice important differences; this is a passive exercise—you do all the work while your partner does nothing at all. Muscles and tendons that are often ignored in a workout are stretched, making the whole upper body more flexible. The smiles usually outlast the stroke, maybe even the whole massage. No pain and plenty of gain.

If your partner has had recent back pain, check with a doctor before flexing the top or bottom part of the back.

During this stroke you will be twisting the whole upper back; first to the right, then to the left. Begin by pushing forward on your partner's right shoulder with the heel of your right hand while you pull back on her left shoulder with your left forearm. Some backs twist much further than others—stop as soon as you run into real resistance.

Back off slowly from the point of tension, and try the movement again. With just three or four repetitions you should feel the point of tension begin to retreat as little-used muscles are gently stretched. Flex the right side of the back four times, then reverse the whole stroke; push forward on your partner's left shoulder with the heel of your left hand while pulling back on her right shoulder with your right forearm.

*Graham, *Massage: Manual Treatment, Remedial Movements*, p. 83.

The Full Back Flex

Since back flexing works best on supple muscles, the period just after exercise is ideal. Athletes are quick to recognize the value of a long stretch that occurs at both ends of the back simultaneously. No exercise can provide this extraordinary effect — it's unique to massage.

Once again, stretching is accomplished by pushing forward with your hand while pulling back with your elbow. When flexing the lower back, however, you're manipulating the whole area from the shoulders to the hips, a much larger part of the body. This doesn't require a great deal more effort than upper back

flexing; nevertheless, a moment or two of careful preparation will definitely make things easier. Before starting the movement, your partner should be reclining on her side, facing away from you and relaxed. If she seems nervous, say a few words about the stroke so she has a general idea of what to expect. First, the hips will move forward while the shoulders move back, then, as you reverse directions, the hips move back while the shoulders come forward. The actual twisting occurs at the top and bottom of the spine.

Start by pulling back on the shoulders while you push forward at the hips. Make a fist, then press your right elbow across the front of your partner's shoulder (as shown). Using the heel of your left hand, push forward gently on the bony crest of your partner's hip. Try to equalize pressures as you push and pull. Usually, the top of the body will move further than the bottom. To compensate for the difference, flex the top and bottom of the body at the same rate until you reach the point of tension at the hips. Then hold steady at the hips and continue twisting at the shoulder. Be especially

careful during this stroke to avoid short, jerky movements. When flexing any part of the body, always move deliberately and slowly.

To flex the back in the other direction there's no need for your partner to move. Simply reverse the hand positions you just used; press forward on the back of her shoulder with the heel of your right hand while pulling back on the hip with your left elbow.

Sometimes, as the joints of the lower back are moved, you will hear a little pop. It's usually followed by a long, satisfied sigh of pleasure.

Flexing the Leg

Flexing the leg effectively stretches out a wide range of lower body muscles where the leg and lower back meet. Near the point of tension every major joint of the lower back will move far enough to extend nearby ligaments — the fibrous bands that connect bones to each other.

With your partner on her side facing away from you, reach straight down and grasp the inside of her bottom leg just above the knee, then reach forward with your other hand into the small of the back. Start slowly so you can carefully equalize the pulling and pushing pressures. Leg flexing requires pressure in two almost opposite directions: pull straight back on the lower leg while pushing forward against the small of the back. If the stroke feels awkward, simply rearrange yourself and your partner. On the first try you will notice that the leg and lower back have different points of tension — adjust your pressures accordingly. Leg flexing stretches

the powerful four-part quadriceps muscles on the front of the thigh. In fact, most of the resistance you feel when pulling back on the leg comes from this large muscle group.

As the bottom leg is flexed, the top leg usually moves forward, bending the back into a graceful arch. Flex the leg three times to the point of tension, then have your partner turn over so you can do the other leg.

Pressing the Leg

With your partner comfortable on her side, it's easy to lift the top leg straight up in the air and press both sides with a squeezing motion. The precise amount that you will be able to lift the leg will of course vary. Never force the leg. As always, massage just inside the point of tension. Supporting the leg with one hand at the ankle leaves the other hand free to squeeze away. Follow the contours of the muscles as you squeeze, avoiding the bony surfaces of the leg and the knee. Move up and down the inside of the leg, squeezing every few inches, then reverse your hands and massage the outside of the leg.

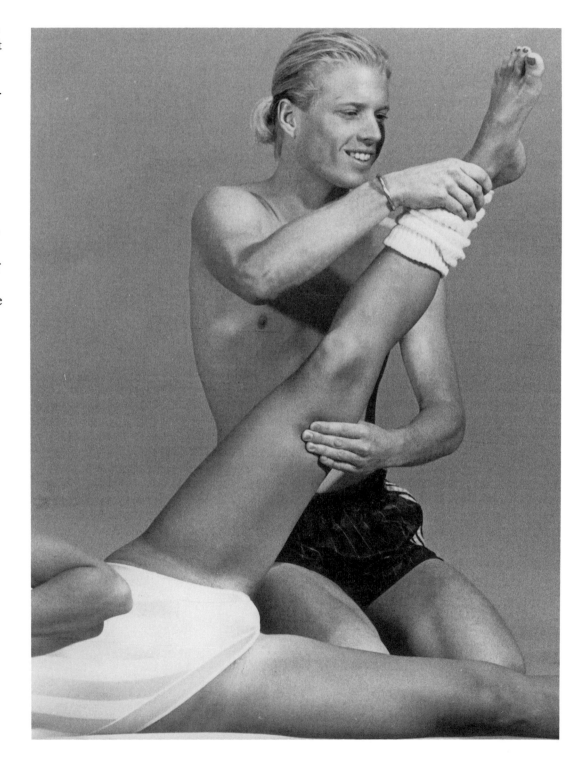

Pumping the Legs

We have all seen the athlete whose earnest exercises are performed within the sad limitations of a body completely dominated by tight muscles. His stride, although vigorous, is short and choppy. Throwing, swimming, or dancing are quirky and unbalanced. In fact, every movement seems to take place in a space that's rigidly defined by perpetually tense muscles. Instead of becoming more supple after exercise, the body merely becomes more obviously stressed. As we have seen, fluid release massage can provide an athlete with a way to transform the exercise experience. Muscle stretching movements,

although not as dramatic, do accomplish something similar: here is a kind of conditioning that your partner simply cannot do as well for himself.

Leg pumping after exercise is a much more energetic movement than the variation used to relieve insomnia. After exercise it's more important to stretch tight muscles, tendons, and ligaments than it is to improve circulation. Leg pumping stretches the large hamstrings on the backs of the thighs, along with a wide range of smaller muscles around the knee. Inside the knee, the body's most complex joint, tiny tendons and

ligaments are extended each time you pump the leg. Note the point of tension on the first pass and pump the leg within its limitations. After a few repetitions the point of tension will usually begin to recede without additional pressure. If it does, don't hesitate to press a bit further as you continue this movement.

With your partner lying on his back, pump one leg first, then the other, and finally, both at once. Lift, using both hands to support your partner's leg above and below the knee, until the knee is straight up. Steady the leg with one hand at the ankle while pressing forward on

the knee with the soft inner part of your forearm (as shown). Lean into this stroke. Hold the leg for a silent count of ten at the point of tension, then release it slowly. It's best to bring the leg all the way back to the full prone starting position. Be sure to provide support above and below the knee as you lower it.

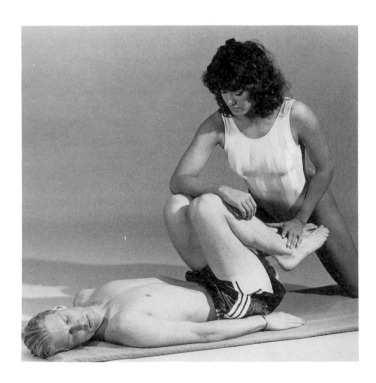 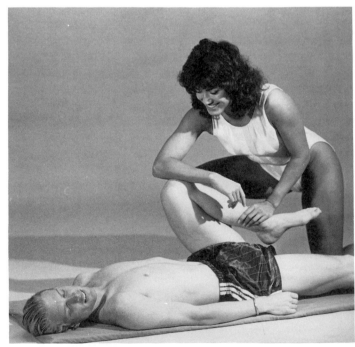

Controlling Cramps

She had played the piano for three and a half hours, too long for her, with the result that the hands and arms were greatly fatigued, and there was twitching of the muscles and rapid, slight contractions of the fingers, alternating with a dull ache, and the whole of both arms felt lame to the shoulders. Under two days of rest alone her symptoms had become worse, and on the morning of the third day, when she first came to me, she could not turn a newspaper nor play a single note on the piano and there was slight swelling of the affected members. Thirty minutes of stroking alternating with deep massage was accompanied and followed by perfect comfort for six hours.
—Douglas Graham, M.D.,
A Treatise on Massage

Legs

Cramping becomes a serious threat the moment the oxygen supply to a muscle drops precipitously. Low temperatures, tight clothing, and excessive exercise can interfere with normal blood circulation. More commonly, however, cramping strikes because stress (and therefore vasoconstriction) has been allowed to continue unchecked. For athletes, the problem usually begins with an overly ambitious workout. If, say, the muscles are not properly warmed up, they can easily fail to meet the extra demands of a long run in cold weather.

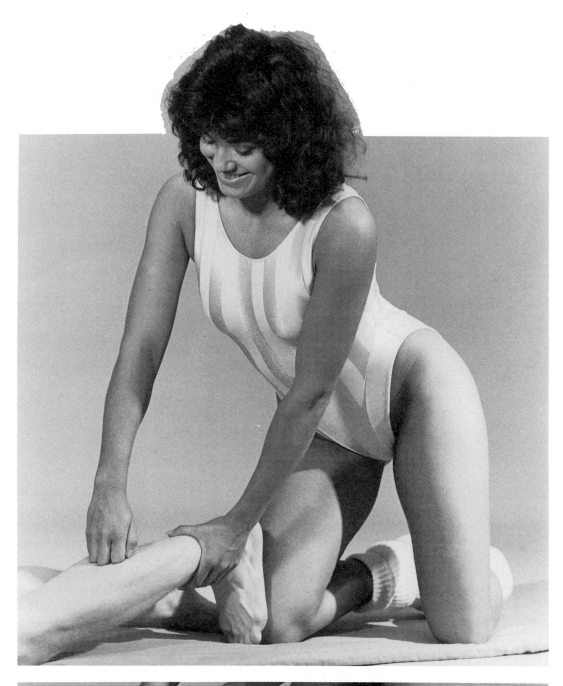

Controlling Cramps (cont'd)

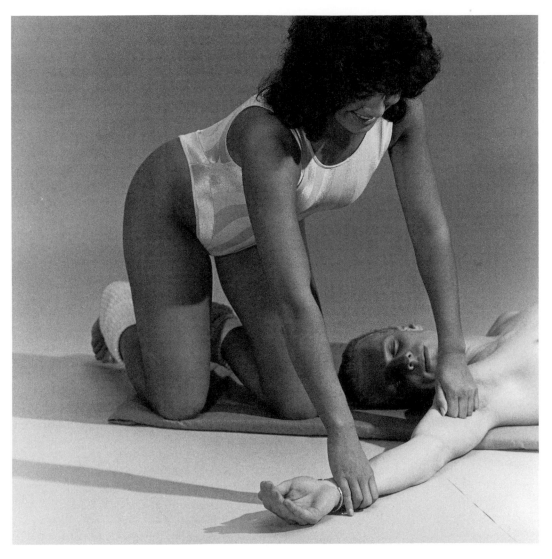

of the muscle. Fingertip knead the whole area (p. 56), then press down with your closed fist and circle with a deep compression movement (p. 67). Try a simple circulation movement (p. 74), pressing blood toward the heart along the whole length of the affected leg. Finish by pulling down from the back of the knee to the ankle with a fast hand-over-hand movement (as shown on p. 129). Squeeze the calf as you pull.

Arms

Stretch out a cramped arm and support it with one hand while you do compression with the other (as shown). Rotate the flat part of your closed fist on the raised muscles of the arm. Stay off exposed blood vessels and the bony shoulder top.

During hand-over-hand pulling, grasp and pull vigorously with each stroke if the muscle has been cramped.

Help your partner rise slowly after the massage — leaping to one's feet the moment the pain diminishes can bring the cramp right back.

Excruciating muscle cramps deliver the message: the leg muscles are out of oxygen.

Most sports-related cramps occur in the arms or legs. Before you attempt any massage, use part of your own body to straighten out the afflicted limb. With your partner lying on his stomach, straighten a cramped calf by pressing your knee hard against the bottom of his foot. Hold it in that position while you massage. Anchor the leg just above the ankle (as shown on p. 129) and press down into the hardened muscle with the flat part of the knuckles. Rotate your hand slowly. Don't stop, even though you may feel the muscle soften as you massage. Move in with friction strokes (p. 32) to the center

Forearm Percussion

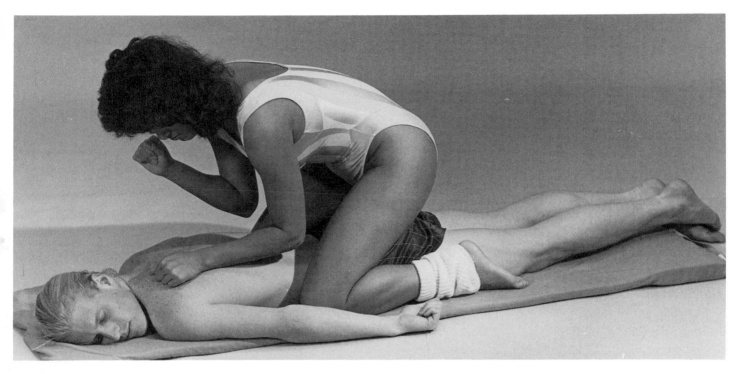

The whole range of percussion strokes becomes useful after exercise, especially if muscle cramping is a problem for your partner. If you can't isolate a specific problem area, a forearm percussion stroke is more generally effective than any of the hands-only variations. The wide muscular center of the back is the perfect place for this movement. Percussion here increases the blood supply to all the vital organs and relaxes the long muscles that run parallel to the spine. By using the whole forearm you substantially increase the contact area, covering half the back with each stroke.

If you're larger than your partner, sit comfortably near his waist but if you're smaller and lighter, try straddling him and sitting back on the hips (as shown). This gives you better balance throughout the stroke and makes reaching forward easier.

Make a fist and, with moderate pressure, snap your whole forearm against your partner's back. Begin on the long muscles that run parallel to the spine and work outward to the sides of the back. The trick is to bring the entire contact surface, from the flat part of the knuckle to the elbow, down at once. Naturally, this stroke will move more slowly than the hands-only percussion movements, but, as always, consistent rhythm is far more important than raw speed.

11.
Instant Energy
at Home
and at Work

Three essential strokes
One minute each, fifty repetitions

☛ Mixed percussion
☛ Fast friction
☛ Walking the back

The Coffee Break Vs. the Massage Break

If your partner has been depending on stimulants for a pickup during the day, massage will open up a new world of possibilities. The following strokes are ideal for hard-working people who want a quick energy boost—without a crash afterward.

In the kitchen, living room, or office, a variety of percussion and friction movements, none of which require oiling or special preparations, can be used to alter your partner's mood. In fact, major changes start happening inside the body even before you finish massaging. In minutes, as oxygen levels throughout the massaged area climb, fatigue is diminished and a wonderfully energetic feeling takes its place. Stiffness in the muscles and joints yields to the sort of fluid ease one usually experiences after a strenuous physical workout. Finally, as acids are flushed out of the tissues to be replaced by oxygen-enriched blood, irritability gives way to an optimistic can-do attitude.

The effects are particularly impressive in situations where people must sit and concentrate for long hours at a telephone, typewriter, or computer. As fatigue departs, endurance levels are dramatically improved. Apple Computer, Pacific Telesis, and Raychem, to name just a few,

Do

Schedule the massage when your partner is not likely to be interrupted. Be punctual.

Get feedback on stroke and pressure preferences.

Appear confident and organized. Bring with you everything you will need.

Take whatever simple steps are possible to quiet the environment.

Take all of your partner's requests seriously.

Leave quietly as soon as the massage is finished.

Don't

Massage while your partner does something else. Don't get flustered if interruptions do occur.

Encourage conversation.

Comment on how tense your partner seems to be.

Randomly explore your partner's body—people dislike being probed.

Impose a complex routine of strokes to impress your partner.

Introduce complicated rules or exotic theories.

Needlessly take up your partner's time.

have already begun regular massage programs for their employees. A masseur visits the office and either moves from desk to desk or massages in a company lounge. Employers and employees alike realize that massage keeps everyone in good spirits while improving productivity.

If you have a few extra minutes during the day, you don't need to hire a professional masseur to relax a tense worker. You can do all of these strokes yourself. At home or at work your reward is that next time you may be the one getting the massage.

If you're pressed for time, however, or have many employees, a good professional masseur is invaluable. But given the wide proliferation of quackery in the field, finding the right masseur or team of masseurs can be tricky. The guidelines that start on p. 142 are designed to help you make the right choice.

Team Massage

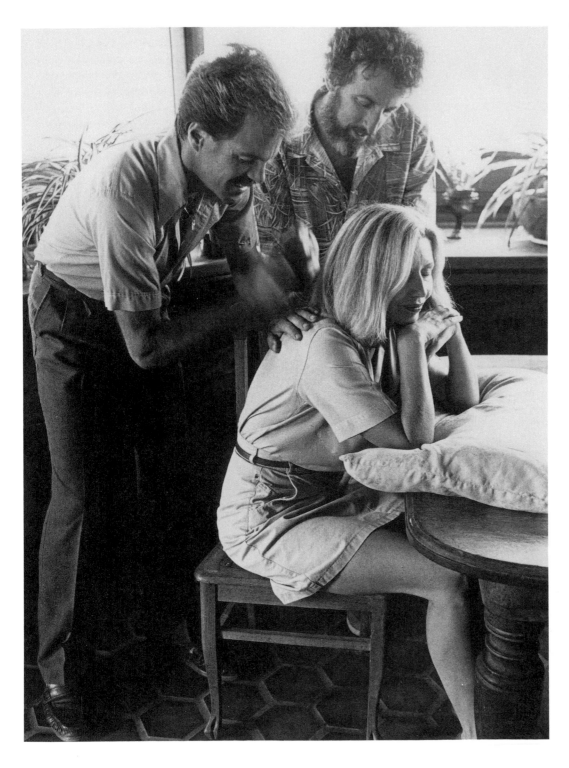

The most common problem one encounters when massaging busy executives is the overbooked itinerary. If your partner is too busy to sit still for a massage, try ganging up on her. Two pairs of hands can deliver twice as much sensation as one. The feeling of *four* hands thundering up and down the back during a pounding movement is so overwhelming that even the most self-absorbed type will stop talking and surrender to massage.

They always thank you afterward.

The Office Pillow

Mixed Percussion

If you can't locate a lounge in which to sprawl out, the massage pillow becomes very important. With it, percussion and friction strokes for the upper back, the staple of on-the-job massage, become much more effective. Every worker needs a pillow large enough to support the full weight of the upper body when placed across the surface of a desk. Subdued colors are most inviting. The pillow should give good support during any of the common percussion movements, but remain firm enough to retain its shape. A removable cover makes occasional oiling possible, although a large towel can serve as well.

Some offices have nothing at all that can be used as a massage pillow, so it's wise to inquire ahead of time and provide one, if necessary, whenever you do massage at work.

Percussion strokes are probably the easiest to prepare for in massage. Don't bother having your partner lie down or remove any clothing; just grab a pillow and you're ready to go. In fact, if no pillow is handy, the head can be supported on the hands without seriously compromising the stroke. For offices without lounges, or for a quick burst of energy around the house, nothing satisfies like a few minutes of intense percussion.

Move up and down the back on both sides of the spine, but stay off the spine itself. Save your greatest pressures for the thickest muscles at the top of the back and across the shoulders. Generally, these movements are more effective over the rib cage, where bones provide a kind of natural cushioning effect. If you move to the lower back, follow the elevated ridge of muscles that runs parallel to the spine. Be careful not to pound on your partner's kidneys. Choose a percussion speed that you can comfortably maintain for a while. Rhythmic consistency is more important than raw speed.

Start with pounding, the most intense percussion movement, and let it give way to a more gentle full hand cupping stroke (see p. 104). A light pinky snap (see p. 105) is nice across the top of the shoulders. Your partner may want to direct the percussion to a specific part of the back; listen for feedback. If nothing is actually said, remember

that pleasurable moaning means that what you're doing feels good—keep it up for a while.

Percussion strokes set up a vibration that carries right through the body. Work on the back for two or three minutes, and the feeling goes on after you stop.

Fast Friction

Raking the Back

Immediately after percussion, while your partner is still relaxing on a pillow, try some fast friction. It's the perfect stroke for that stiff neck or nagging pain at the top of the back. This energetic, immensely versatile friction variation can be used on almost every part of the body. It penetrates easily through clothing and works in nearly any setting, making it ideal for on-the-job massage. Fast friction is one of the rare massage strokes that takes some real effort to sustain. However, the extra exertion is always appreciated; no other stroke in massage produces a more intense feeling. It's shown here on the top of the back, the area most frequently requested by office workers, but the stroke is equally effective on any fleshy part of the body.

The key to successful fast friction is good anchoring, without which the movement becomes sloppy and random. To cover the whole upper back, push down between the shoulder blades with the flat surface of one hand, then work up to the lower neck (as shown). Anchor near the shoulder, pushing flesh toward your friction hand. You'll need to reposition your anchor hand frequently during fast friction. Rotate the friction hand while pressing down moderately hard. Remember: friction strokes turn on the interior tissues, not the surface of the skin. You will feel the muscular interior of the upper back as you turn. Press in constantly with your anchor hand to confine the movement to the area under your friction hand — you don't want to shake the entire body. Your partner should feel an intense vibration that is confined to a single spot. Once you get the feel of the stroke, try increasing the speed. Fast friction can move almost as fast as you're able to go, but never push it to the limit — you'll have trouble sustaining the speed and controlling the stroke. Check with your partner to find out just how much speed he likes.

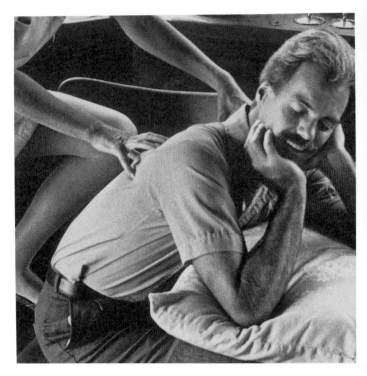

Generally, most massage strokes stay off the spine itself, focusing instead on nearby muscle groups. Whenever they get tight, the long muscles that run parallel to the spine pull directly on spinal nerves. Repeated frequently enough, this stroke will go a long way toward relieving direct muscle pressure to the spine that keeps the nerves irritated.

Have your partner lean forward and support the weight of his head either on his arms or a desktop pillow. Forming a rigid arch with both hands, begin stroking down both sides of the spine with your fingertips. Keep your fingers flexed and rigid throughout this stroke. That way you can glide across the surface of clothing while penetrating deep within. Start at the neck and pull straight down in a series of alternating, foot-long strokes. The stroke moves slowly down the back, covering every portion five or six times. When you reach the bottom of the spine, start again from the top. Rake the whole back at least three times.

Walking the Back

Traditional back walking works only if you're considerably smaller and lighter than your partner. With a bit more effort much the same effect can be created using the fists. In fact, you can feel tensions with the hands that would go unnoticed beneath the feet. As your hands travel up and down the back, pressures can be directed with great precision—you can actually feel tensed muscles begin to relax.

This movement follows the same path you took during the raking stroke. You can stand directly behind your partner and do both sides of the spine at once (as shown). Make a fist and press the flat part of the knuckle into the long muscles that run parallel to the spine. As your fist sinks into the muscle, roll it forward slightly, pressing down hard as you roll. Start at the base of the neck with one fist, then repeat the movement immediately below with the other. Move all the way down the spine, pressing down first with one fist, then the other. Do each side of the spine twice; more if your partner asks for it.

They usually do.

Quick Friction
for the Arms and Hands

Although the hands and arms are used constantly at work, we tend to ignore their aches and pains, focusing instead on the shoulders or lower back. Given just five minutes to work, most masseurs will settle for the lower back and shoulders. Before you do, look closely at your partner's job. Are typing, computer

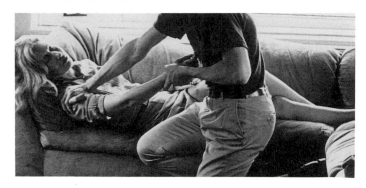

work, or extended telephone conversations required? After massage, the feeling of new-found energy will be just as invigorating in the hands and arms as in the high stress areas of the back.

This stroke also provides an excellent introduction to on-the-job massage. Even the most harried executive can be persuaded to rest an arm on the desk for a few minutes, or better yet, collapse on a couch in the company lounge.

Remember: you need only a few minutes to get the fluid release effect started. With your partner lying on her back, anchor her extended arm at the wrist (as shown) and press down on the fore-arm with the flat surface of your knuckle. Rotate slowly, moving up and down the arm from the wrist to the shoul-

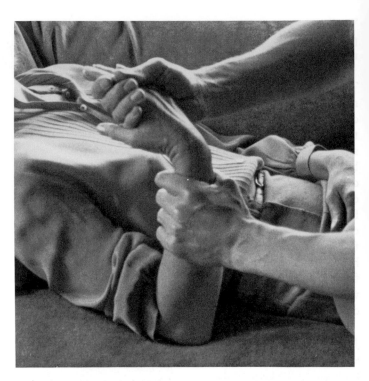

der. Ease up over the exposed blood vessels at the wrist and inside the elbow, reserving your real pressures for the muscular forearm.

To massage the shoulders, circle your partner's wrist and pull it straight out until the whole arm is extended (as shown). Then rotate the same flat part of your knuckle on the muscular shoulder top.

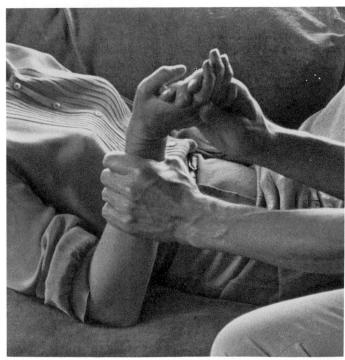

Rotating the Bones
of the Arm and Hand

When was the last time your partner had her bones rotated?

The hand is operated by remote control via long tendons and bones that begin at the elbow. As the hand and arm turn, the two descending bones, the radius and ulna, demonstrate one of the more extraordinary aspects of human anatomy by actually crossing at the center of the forearm. During massage, however, the bones of the forearm can be made to cross while simply rotating the complex joint at the wrist.

Just as an effective foot massage starts up at the knee, massage for the hand must consider parts of the body between the wrist and elbow. Grasp your partner's hand around her loosely clenched fingers (as shown on p. 138) and rotate the wrist once just to test the limits of the turning arc. Pay close attention to the real limits of the arc, which will change several times in a single rotation. As you turn the wrist, the bones of the forearm will cross and uncross themselves.

Rotate the hand three times in each direction. Then grasp your partner's hand tightly between both of your hands, keeping your thumbs on top (as shown) and rotate your hands slowly. The bones inside her hand will move with your hands. Massaging on a couch, you can rotate the bones of her other hand by simply reaching across her body. There's no need for your partner to move at any time during this stroke. You do all the work for her.

Throwing the Arm

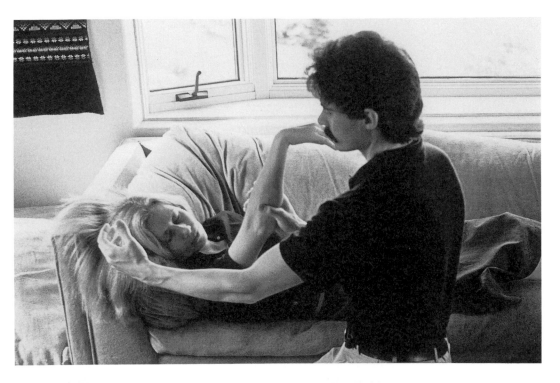

Here is the perfect movement to break the monotony of desk work. While an arm flies through the air, your partner does nothing at all. The large ball joint at the shoulder is vigorously exercised as circulation throughout the limb is stimulated.

Lift your partner's arm first above the elbow (as shown), then at the wrist, until it's straight up in the air. Continuing to hold steady at the wrist, bring the arm up over her head until you feel resistance. Then move the wrist and arm all the way down to a point near her waist. Move the arm back and forth several times until you are completely familiar with the limits of the arc. Only then are you ready to begin the throwing part of the movement, starting with a small arc and enlarging it gradually. With your partner's arm fully extended, toss the wrist from one hand to the other. As you increase your throwing arc to the previously established limits, increase the speed. Let your arm give way a bit each time you catch your partner's wrist. Reach across your partner's body to throw the other arm.

This is the fastest passive exercise. Arm throwing—a thriller.

Real and Imaginary Massage

Our Puritan heritage has assigned all physical contact between adults to two rather narrow categories: sexual or commercial. You're either making a sexual advance or you're making money when you touch other adults. Those engaged in commercial touching are careful to remain as impersonal as possible lest they be accused of making a sexual advance. This unfortunate stereotyping has created serious confusion in the massage profession. We have massage as a familiar euphemism for prostitution vs. massage therapy in which the body is manipulated as impersonally as a collection of auto parts. Real massage, the kind that has been practiced everywhere on earth since biblical times, is a sensual art: it works because it feels good. Sensuality is part of the wide spectrum of human feeling between sex and therapy. We live in a society that tries to deny its existence.

In massage, this denial has created some bizarre imitations. A prostitute posing as masseuse fiddles around with a leg or an arm for a minute or two before getting down to business. The customer really didn't expect massage and none was offered. But the massage therapist posing as doctor has even less use for real massage. Any gadget that will confer authority on the

practitioner and distance him from the sensual is embraced wholeheartedly. High-speed electrical devices, magnets, bits of stone, and vials of uncertain chemicals are solemnly pressed against the body. Hands are waved back and forth in the air in order to "balance" mysterious forces.

When flesh finally does meet flesh, it's always to demonstrate an exotic theory, never simply to please. Bursts of nasty finger-poking alternate with violent manipulation of the joints because "blocked energy" must be liberated. Strokes wander aimlessly across the body, departing from the map of the circulatory system, from nerve paths, and, finally, from all known systems. As the confusion mounts, charts covered with exotic oriental characters are rolled out, indicating that dozens of independent lines converge on the bottom of the spine, the side of an ear, or the back of one toe. And of course the magnets and bits of stone converge on

those spots with full liturgical ceremony.

Through it all the practitioner advances relentlessly on his helpless "patient," self-righteously poking, jabbing, and pulling at the body in the name of "healing." In manner, if not in practice, the therapist seeks to emulate the high priests of the medical profession (usually his sworn enemies). Ask a question and the authoritative bullying begins: your therapist knows things you don't know about: "meridians," "auras," "energy imbalances," and "pressure points." It's all very mysterious and complex, and if it hurts, well . . . it's good for you.

Quackery, not prostitution, is the biggest problem facing massage today. We're in the process of rediscovering an ancient health principle that can enrich our lives, but for many people the quack and his spooky bag of tricks will be the first and last contact with massage. The human

body, perhaps the most complex arrangement of matter in nature, remains a mystery to the quack. He usually has little understanding of anatomy and no appreciation for the simple, sensual beauty of massage. Those who love massage understand that something primal pervades the experience — this is one of the most ancient human activities. Unfortunately, so is quackery.

Thousands of years ago, when people massaged by the light of open fires, bead strokers and body pokers concentrated on purging the body of evil spirits. Proving? That, in quackery, little has changed over the past few millenniums; self-promotion remains far more important than healing. The quack has always sought power by transforming the body into a supernatural freak show that only he can understand.

But there is a gray zone, too, between quackery and real massage. Many earnest practitioners, concerned that their efforts will be confused with prostitution, go to great lengths to "dignify" massage. The airs and exotic terminology are usually abandoned the moment a partner begins to sink into that profound state of relaxation that only real massage can bring.

How to Find a Good Professional Masseur

Thinking of hiring a professional masseur for yourself or your company? The rewards are great, but it pays to shop carefully.

The right masseur, or team of masseurs, can change the whole working environment for a small or large company. Employees are happier, more relaxed; the workplace becomes a pleasant environment where one feels good. Absenteeism declines, and productivity, that elusive goal, goes up. Do something this nice for your employees, and they're going to return the favor.

How much is stress costing you? Are your employees attempting to tack ambitious exercise programs onto the workload—failing—then turning to drugs to relax? Professional massage is less expensive and time-consuming than any of the standard medical services. You'll see dramatic results after just five minutes of massage two or three times a week; each session takes less time than the average coffee break. If stress is a serious problem at your company, massage can become a kind of preventive medicine, permitting the doctor to do other things. Which would you rather pay: the masseur or the workman's compensation claims?

The number of good professional masseurs is growing every year, but with no standardized licensing procedures, you have no way of knowing what to expect until the massage begins. Nevertheless, setting up a corporate massage program is one of the most pleasant tasks in business, simply because the interviewer will be massaged by so many of the job applicants. But there's more to the interviewing job than collapsing on a couch in your office while your neck and shoulders are kneaded. Use the following guidelines to pick the right professional for your company.

First, find out if any companies in your area have already set up massage programs—their recommendations are a good place to begin. Larger companies require a team of masseurs with a common philosophy— a program. Choose a program that's flexible enough to fit into your business day. If there's no separate lounge area in your company that can be used for massage, a team should be able to adapt to conditions in the office itself without causing any problems. If necessary, massage can be going on at one desk while work proceeds at the next. Again, the best way to audition a masseur, once

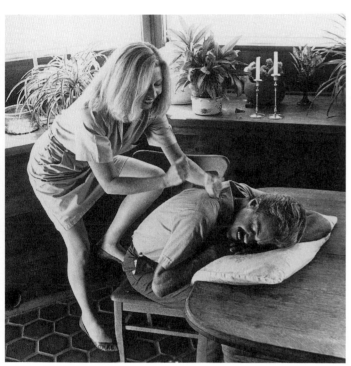

The Massage Bill of Rights

You have the right:

To remain silent and to expect the same from your masseur.

To refuse phone calls or other interruptions.

To uninterrupted pleasure throughout a massage.

To walk out if the massage is unpleasant.

To direct the massage, requesting specific strokes and timings if you so desire.

To be warm and comfortable.

To choose the music if you're in the mood for music.

To be alone afterward.

references have been checked and preliminary interviews completed, is on your own body. Each masseur should be able to continue any stroke for at least five minutes without breaking rhythm. Ideally, he (or she) should be as efficient and invisible as a good waiter. And as silent.

If you're planning an extended massage program for a larger company, hire masseurs who keep simple records concerning the condition and special needs of each employee. Finally, look closely at your masseur's general presentation. A calm, confident manner will help put your employees at ease,

while an officious, overly busy approach will ruin the experience. A masseur should be clean, with carefully trimmed fingernails, and a pleasant personality.

How do you separate the quacks from the serious masseurs? *Beware of any practitioner who attempts to justify painful treatments in the name of massage.* The quack shows up with an incomprehensible program that invariably includes plenty of nasty poking and twisting "because it's good for you." At best the quack is annoying and a waste of time, at worst actually dangerous. Turn one loose in your office, and your

employees become a testing ground for excruciating "body therapies," thereby creating more, not less, work for the company doctor. The responsible practitioner, on the other hand, will respect your rights throughout a massage (see "The Massage Bill of Rights"). It is, after all, your body, not a pet theory, that matters most. Above all a masseur must be flexible enough to meet your personal needs. This means that you should get exactly what *you* desire (even if it means skipping the masseur's forty-seven-point program). If you want your shoulders kneaded for five minutes straight, ask, and if you get an argument, move on to another masseur.

Much the same criteria can be used to hire a personal masseur. Naturally, it becomes even more important to be sure the masseur will be sensitive to your own specialized needs. People come in various body types, and a good masseur will recognize yours, immediately seeking out the trouble spots and lingering on the most pleasure-sensitive areas. Nevertheless, your requests, if you feel like making any, should come first. And afterward you should feel much more relaxed than before.

12.
A Ten-Minute
Erotic Massage

Three essential strokes
One minute each, fifty repetitions

☞ Local circulation
☞ Pumping the legs
☞ A full body stroke

Banishing the After-Work Blues: The Sex Enhancer

. . .why do I yield to that
* suggestion*
whose horrid image doth unfix
* my hair*
And make my seated heart
* knock at*
my ribs against the use of
* nature?*
Present fears are less than
* horrible imaginings.*
—William Shakespeare,
Macbeth

If the mind is the greatest aphrodisiac, then fear and tension are the principal enemies of good sex. We yield to our fears when we're over-tired and overstressed. Without relaxation and the trust that follows, good sex is rare. The familiar "after-work blues," a combination of headaches, muscular aches and pains, and general irritability, can easily turn sex into a joyless chore. The trick is to find a way to leave your problems, anxieties, and fears at the office so they don't end up in bed. You must find a way to relax after work without working at it.

The after-work blues, like other stress-related complaints, originate in the body, not the mind. Deal with the physical manifestations of stress, and the emotional problems, which may seem terribly deep-seated, begin to disappear. Has your partner been sitting for long periods with little opportunity for

Focusing your erotic massage

Does the base of the neck or the lower back hurt?
Is your partner in pain from a recent accident?
Has your partner been wearing tight shoes?
Can you see visible marks from tight clothing?
Does your partner complain of being continually overstressed?
Is your partner taking stimulants or tranquilizers?
Is your partner wearing contact lenses?
Is there a hot bath or shower near your massage area?
Can you eliminate telephone calls and visitors?
Are children and pets cared for?

any kind of exercise? Has constant scheduling pressure reduced him to a nervous wreck? Have many arguments occurred?

If the answer to any one of these questions is yes, you can be certain that concentrated acidic wastes are trapped in the tissues. Inside the body the hidden source of most stress is usually marked by a peculiar concentration of nasty chemicals. With or without drugs, it is virtually impossible for anyone to relax while the muscles are bathed in lactic and carbonic acids. To vanquish the after-work blues, you must get rid of those acids. If you don't, there's no hope for real relaxation. And not much chance for good sex.

If the acids are hidden, their effects certainly are not. You can usually anticipate the quality of a sexual encounter by simply observing your partner's mood before sex. Look carefully at the response to tension after an exhausting day at work. Do you see a general collapse on a comfortable chair with a cocktail or three (just enough to take the edge off, you understand)? Sex after heavy drinking will be tense because alcohol doesn't bring true relaxation, it simply depresses the nervous system. And turning off the mind

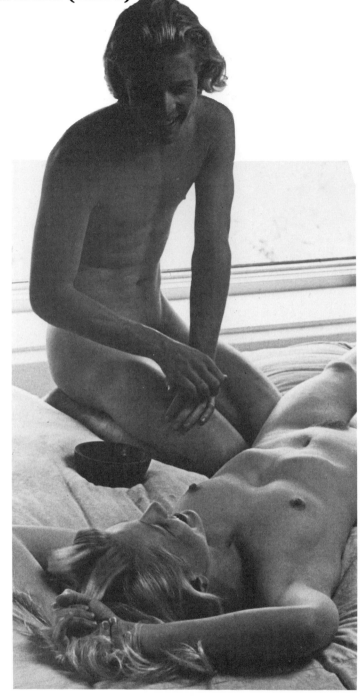

with vast stretches of uninterrupted TV doesn't get rid of a stiff neck, lower back pain, or congested feelings in the legs. Selected tranquilizers may distance one from various pains (for a while) and from sexual desire as well, but in a few hours, when the tranquilizers wear off, all of the discomfort returns with an extra measure of anxiety. And good sex is more remote than ever.

Should sex itself be reduced to a vehicle for releasing tension, a kind of rudimentary physical therapy for burned-out bodies? That approach transforms the "therapist" into a martyr, an unwilling, even resentful, sexual partner. Happily, you can find a better way.

Your partner can experience an extraordinary release from tension after just a brief fluid release sequence. The massage will immediately become much more real than any fears or anxieties. As you massage, real relaxation courses through the body, the muscles become receptive instead of resistant, and, in minutes, the after-work blues suddenly vanish. This, of course, is precisely the kind of "instant" relief that's promised by painkillers and tranquiliz-

ers, but somehow never quite delivered. With Super Massage it's easy to scrupulously clear internal wastes from the tissues, then oxygenate the entire stressed area. Here is a quick way to vanquish the after-work blues and present your partner with an exceedingly considerate gift: drug-free relaxation; an easy transition from anxiety to blessed peace. At the end of a long day give your partner a massage instead of a drink or pill.

This is not an argument for tacking on a few minutes of massage as a kind of extra foreplay to help seduce the unwilling. Use massage as a two-stage sex enhancer. One, as a means for relaxing your partner and clearing acidic irritants from the body. Two, as a part of sex itself. Ideally, in part one, massage should be separated from foreplay and sex, lest it be viewed as manipulative by a stressed-out partner. Never make demands on your partner during massage. Massage is not sexual ammunition. Instead, see it as a means for transforming an exhausted, stressed-out body. With massage, you focus on the entire body, not just the so-called erogenous zones. Afterward, one feels pampered, perhaps even a bit spoiled. And once relaxation comes, all else becomes possible.

Your partner's not ready for sex if he or she is:

Argumentative.
Rushed.
Having trouble sitting still (compulsive foot tapping, teeth grinding).
Sitting with one leg wrapped around the other.
Complaining of vague aches and pains.
Accident prone.
Unable to concentrate.
Constantly talking about work.
Pale or out of breath. Exhausted.

Reducing Erotic Stress: Local Circulation

Pressing blood back toward the heart on all the limbs accomplishes several things at once. First, your partner's blood pressure is lowered — you're doing some of the work usually done by the heart. Secondly, the massaged limb is oxygenated, which leaves it feeling light and energetic. Most important, however, your partner experiences a new kind of touch. Perhaps for the first time since childhood somebody else is paying attention to, say, the lower leg. Forget the so-called erogenous zones and concentrate instead on basic sensory awareness. The arms can be a source of great pleasure. So can the legs and the feet.

Begin at the wrists on the arms, or at the ankles on the legs. Wrap your hands around one limb, making contact from the base of the palms to the fingertips. Move up toward the top of the limb, using the hands-opposed position common to all circulation strokes. Turn at the top of the limb and descend along the sides (as shown), making contact all the way back to the starting point. The pressure part of this stroke is always on the way up, toward the heart.

Reducing Erotic Stress:
Fast Stroking the Knee

The knee is the most complex joint in the body. Its smooth operation depends on keeping supple both the tendons that connect muscles to the knee and the ligaments that connect bones within the knee. This becomes difficult if the large muscles above and below the knee are perpetually tense. But once you've massaged the whole leg and the large muscle groups begin to relax, the knee will benefit from a fast stroking movement that makes things happen inside the complex web of ligaments, blood vessels, and tendons.

Use two contact points for this movement: on the fleshy back of the knee and just below the kneecap itself. With fingers pressed together, lift up slightly on the bottom of the knee with both hands, then slide the sides of your thumbs into the groove just below the kneecap. Stroke back and forth with your fingers under the knee while your thumbs make light contact above. One hand moves forward while the other moves back. With a little practice, great bursts of speed behind the knee are fun. As you build up speed, you can sometimes actually feel the warmth generated by your hands. So can your partner.

Reducing Erotic Stress:
Forearm Compression

Does your partner worry too much about sex? Curiously, erotic stress seems to generate tension in the muscles of the calf. If nothing is done to relieve the tension, excruciating calf cramps, which usually strike suddenly in the cold hours of the early morning, will follow. Here is a stroke that flexes the leg while you relax all of its major muscle groups. Forearm compression travels well, spreading very pleasant sensations up and down your partner's leg all the while.

Oil the inside of your forearm before starting. Use extra oil if you have hairy arms. Begin on the thigh, then move down to the inside of the calf. Lift your partner's leg with both hands (always use two hands when moving a limb), then hold it in place with one hand just above the ankle (as shown). Lean forward, make a fist, and press down against the front of her thigh with the fleshy part of your forearm. Circle as you press. Move slowly up and down the thigh until you have covered the whole area between the knee and hip at least three times. Then, without breaking the compression

rhythm, move down to the inside of the calf.

Turn your forearm so the same fleshy inner surface makes contact with your partner's calf. Once the knee is raised, the calf will become much more relaxed than the thigh was. Nevertheless, you can often feel tension draining out of the muscles as you

massage. Press down into the muscle tissue and begin rotating your forearm. On this part of the body you can travel all the way from the ankle to the back of the knee. Here again, make at least three passes over the entire lower leg. To complete the movement, use both hands to provide support above and below the knee, then slowly lower your partner's leg to the massage surface.

Reducing Erotic Stress: Pumping the Leg

Pumping the leg flexes joints at the knee and hip and helps to stretch out a quirky lower back. Don't be surprised if your partner sighs with pleasure when you're through.

With your partner lying on her back, position yourself so you can easily reach the center of her body. Then,

using both hands, lift one leg (as shown). While steadying the leg with one hand around the middle of the calf, press forward just below the knee with the fleshy inside of your other forearm. The point of tension, the spot where you encounter resistance, will vary. Feel for it the first time you press forward and don't

press far past that point on successive strokes. A slight stretch feels good, but be careful not to force your partner into an uncomfortable position.

Pump each leg at least four times.

Awakening the Body:
A Full Body Stroke

Pure deepening whirlpools of sensation swirling deeper and deeper through all her tissue and consciousness, til she was one perfect concentric fluid of feeling. —D.H. Lawrence, *Lady Chatterly's Lover*

In massage we think of the erotic strokes as a gentle way of opening certain doors — the experience may or may not culminate in actual sex. Therapists have begun experimenting with erotic massage in the hopes of offering highly stressed couples an attractive alternative to lovemaking that has degenerated into a furious race to orgasm. First, couples are encouraged to relax and simply make physical contact with each other. No drugs, no pressure to perform — just touching. But the touching is educated, not random; circulation is boosted, aches and pains vanish, a joint becomes more supple.

People who have lived together for years discover, perhaps for the first time, each other's knees, feet, and scalp. Gradually, of course, the nonthreatening physical contact becomes a delightful little time bomb. You can use the same techniques that work for couples on a single highly stressed partner, but be aware that this is a very powerful tool. At its best, a first erotic massage can come close to redefining the sexual act.

Try to avoid conversation during an erotic massage. Now, more than ever before, words will come between your partner and the feeling. Conversation will almost always bring on a certain anxiety, which cheats both partners and generates even more stress. The secret of erotic massage is the gratifying way it can expand the range of feeling before sex. In just a few minutes your partner will experience what he or she has been missing. And of course the strokes are just as effective on a relaxed partner who simply wants to feel more.

Erotic massage works best on a firm bed or warm, well-padded massage surface. Surely the bedroom is the one place where we should all be completely free. But we struggle, even there, with each other's desires; the anti-tactile legacy of Puritanism manages to intrude on our most private moments. Expecting erotic feelings to be confined to the immediate area around the genitals,

A Full Body Stroke (cont'd)

we abandon the other 95 percent of the body during foreplay and sex. But not during erotic massage . . .

To soothe the nerves, you massaged the whole back of the body. Now you can massage the entire front of the body with a single movement that passes over most of the well-known erogenous zones. Erotic massage is supremely democratic; a breast should receive no more attention than a shoulder. By not stopping, not emphasizing the obviously erotic, you can make some electrifying connections. As you press up the legs, your partner waits with terrific anticipation and then . . . your hands move on. The moment you pass over a traditional erotic zone, the familiar intense feelings spread to the next part of the body. A feeling of excitement builds as you massage; it travels with your hands. Erotic massage animates the whole body and turns it into an instrument of pleasure.

First, oil her entire body. With your partner lying on her back, start on the front of the ankles with your hands wrapped over your partner's legs, fingers facing each other. Throughout this stroke, try to make contact with the

whole surface of your hand, from the fingertips to the base of the palm. Push up the legs slowly, allowing your hands to flatten out above the knees to meet the broad expanse of the thigh (as shown on p. 151). Use moderate pressures. Be

prepared to reposition your body several times as you move up from the feet to the shoulders. (Try not to interrupt the movement.) At the waist your fingertips will nearly meet. Press up to the very top of the torso and turn

out over the shoulder tops, allowing your hands to follow the precise contours of the shoulders (as shown). Turn in at the armpit and, with your fingertips pointed straight down and your fingers pressed tightly together, pull down the side of the torso and legs to the feet. Turn again at the ankles, maintaining maximum contact right through the turn, until your hands are back in the starting position.

This is the longest continual stroke in massage. Be especially careful not to rush any part of it. What your partner feels is a delicious wave of sensation sweeping back and forth across the body. Be generous. Let the feeling go on.

Awakening the Body: The Full Body Lift

Is your partner skeptical about the power of massage? This is the stroke to begin with even if you're planning to do only two or three others.

The spectacular full body lift is usually employed to flex the spine and lower back, but it has a very useful side effect for headache sufferers; large quantities of oxygen-enriched blood are moved down into the head. Here is a fast way to get oxygen into the brain by simply dumping it there. The full body lift also permits your partner to experience being lifted entirely off the ground by another person, perhaps for the first time since childhood. In fact, if you can hold your partner up for a full minute, you will see an unmistakable difference afterward. The face appears ruddy, almost flushed, and some of the tension lines around the eyes and mouth have already vanished. This is one of the rare massage strokes where physical strength is important. Obviously, if your partner is a great deal larger than you, a full body lift will be awkward. Fast stroking the neck (see p. 46) will accomplish the same thing — you'll just need a bit more time.

If size is no problem, don't miss the full body lift. The effect is dramatic and nearly instantaneous. Lift from a tripod position, with one knee and foot down, and the other knee up (as shown). Clasp your fingers together basket style under the small of your partner's back. Then lift slowly, allowing her head to fall back gracefully. Pause at the top of the lift for about thirty seconds. You may want to reach forward with one hand and support her head as you lower her. Don't break contact if you're going to lift a second or third time. With her eyes closed, your partner will experience the lifts as a single uninterrupted movement during which she floats up and down into space.

Awakening the Body:
Hair Brushing

*A strand of your hair touches
  my cheek.
How much better for the
  world had nothing else ever
  happened in it.*
— Kenneth Patchen, "The
Great Birds"

The luxurious feeling of animal fur only approximates
the real thing: human hair.
People love being touched by
each other's hair, but seldom
have an opportunity to experience it. Did we turn to ani-
mals and their furry coats
because we couldn't depend
on each other? Give your partner the chance to change all
that by using your hair as part
of the massage.

You don't need very long hair
to do this stroke; with care,
just a few inches will work
nicely. Hair brushing usually
has to be done from a kneeling position, which may be
difficult to hold for long
periods. Nevertheless, even a
half minute of this delicious
sensation will enhance any
erotic sequence. Kneel near
the center of the area you
want to cover and lower your
head until the top is nearly
parallel to your partner's
body. It helps to rest on both
hands whenever you need to
lean forward (as shown).
Then, let your hair fall,
slowly, onto naked skin.
Move up and down the body,
keeping your head in the
same position. Hair brushing
is a long, leisurely stroke that
can cover the entire body.
Make it last.

An Extended Erotic Massage

An epicurean who wishes to follow the ancient Greek model doesn't simply wallow in sensuality but rather distances himself from the world in order to experience pleasure more fully. We all understand why music sounds better in a symphony hall than a cafeteria; to really know a beautiful thing you must first remove unnecessary distractions. The epicurean isolates a pleasure; then, at his leisure, enjoys its essence.

No society in recorded history has offered greater opportunities for the pleasure lover than ours. Nevertheless, stress levels continue to climb. We have seen how pure sensual pleasure can relax the body and provide quick relief from stress. But when was the last time your partner allowed himself just fifteen minutes of pure sensual pleasure? Perhaps our pleasures are elusive precisely because we fail to follow the epicurean example. We are surrounded by an array of glittering toys; the trick is to play with them properly.

Most professional masseurs will recognize the client who specializes in a wholly materialistic approach to pleasure. Every sensation becomes a kind of possession — tasted

for a moment, then discarded in the greedy rush for new experience. But purely sensual pleasure can't be rushed, compressed, or collected.

Make that point with your hands during erotic massage by creating feelings that will reach any human being on the most profoundly personal level. An extended erotic massage can redefine your partner's whole concept of pleasure.

To establish the right mood, begin with long unhurried stroking movements (see p. 37) repeated dozens of times. Watch the pleasure register from one end of the body to the other as tensed muscles relax beneath your hands. Closing his eyes, your partner abandons the familiar senses and settles into the most private place of all — the body itself. Soon the clock stops and pure sensation takes over. The best erotic massage takes place in a world of its own, the exquisitely private world of touch where everything that is known is simply felt.

The traditional erogenous zones, a mere 5 or 10 percent of the whole body, exclude nearly everything beyond the sex organs themselves. Massage offers you the chance to break out of these ungenerous restrictions by turning the entire body into an instrument of pleasure. Taking the time to extend the limits of erotic feeling introduces your partner to an essential sensual experience: pure pleasure from head to toe. Extend the massage and the feeling will continue.

5

MASSAGE AND
LIFE EXTENSION

13.
Stress, Aging, and Massage

And after she had bathed him and annointed him with olive oil, and cast about him a goodly mantle, he came forth from the bath in fashion like the deathless gods. — Homer, *The Odyssey*

A Regular Program of Massage

Thanks to research on the fluid release effect, we know precisely how powerful massage can be. In minutes, pain is transformed into pleasure, and fatigue gives way to feelings of great energy. Muscle recovery rates after exercise increase so dramatically that one almost has to experience the effect to believe it. And every part of the body that is massaged becomes totally animated, perhaps for the first time since childhood. Whether it lasts a few minutes or several hours, the massage experience is one of continuous pleasure. Expect no unpleasant aftereffects; no secret price must be paid.

Nevertheless, all of these wonderful effects are temporary. The chemical changes inside the body such as increased oxygen supply, more efficient combustion and elimination of wastes, more supple joints and muscles, have been observed as long as one full week after a thorough massage session. Then they vanish.

We have seen how stress can literally kill people. And perhaps by now a few readers have experienced, firsthand, the way massage can be used to control, even eliminate stress. The question is: what if one were massaged all the time? Hippocrates, who had himself massaged daily, lived

to the age of 104. Could it have been the massage that kept him going?

We have come a long way since the golden age of Greece — with the same bodies. As millions of people struggle to cope with stress that seems to come from all quarters, the speedy space age could degen-erate into the pill age. The differences between us and the Hunzas, perhaps the most long-lived people on earth, are instructive. They live in a beautiful place with little noise, pollution, or crime. Rushing, for its own sake, is virtually unknown. The Hunzas also have an extremely stable family structure. In

short, as a society, they are far less stressed than we are.

Of course we cannot hope to duplicate the utopian environment of the Hunzas, but we can look closely at the lives of very old people in our own society. Not surprisingly, a similar low stress pattern emerges: they don't worry

A Regular Program (cont'd)

too much, they know how to relax, and they aren't angry all the time. In fact, even in the most chaotic societies certain individuals somehow manage to stay relatively peaceful. And relatively stress free.

A program of *daily* massage is not part of any major health plan, but it is, perhaps, the missing link in the modern health equation. Diet, exercise, and massage. Over the past few years we have seen a tremendous surge of interest in fitness-oriented exercise, and today our parks are filled with determined runners.

Athletes, we are told, will probably live longer. A scientific evaluation of the relationship between massage and longevity would, of course, take years to reach a conclusion. *But what if it were clearly demonstrated that frequent mas-*

sage, by ridding the body of various wastes and toxins, super-oxygenating the tissues, and lowering stress levels does, in fact, slow the aging process?

Can we expect a massage renaissance to equal the fitness craze? Will the parks and beaches ten or twenty years from now be filled with massaging couples? Will massage be taught to children at home and in school? We have "fat farms," what about massage farms? Will we see daily team massage lasting perhaps several hours for stroke and nervous breakdown victims? Will massage-medicine clinics take their place beside sports-medicine and other specialized facilities? Will regular massage actually extend one's life?

Stay tuned.